Conflicting Legal Cultures in Commercial Arbitration

Old Issues and New Trends

STUDIES IN COMPARATIVE CORPORATE AND FINANCIAL LAW

Volume 4

Series Editor

Barry Rider
Institute of Advanced Legal Studies
University of London
Charles Clore House
17 Russell Square
London WC1 5DR

The titles published in this series are listed at the end of this volume

Conflicting Legal Cultures in Commercial Arbitration

Old Issues and New Trends

Stefan N. Frommel and Barry A.K. Rider (eds.)

INSTITUTE OF ADVANCED LEGAL STUDIES

KLUWER LAW INTERNATIONAL
THE HAGUE – LONDON – BOSTON

Published by
Kluwer Law International Ltd
Sterling House
66 Wilton Road
London SW1V 1DE
United Kingdom

Sold and distributed
in the USA and Canada by
Kluwer Law International
675 Massachusetts Avenue
Cambridge MA 02139
USA

Kluwer Law International incorporates
the publishing programmes of
Graham & Trotman Ltd,
Kluwer Law & Taxation Publishers
and Martinus Nijhoff Publishers

In all other countries, sold and distributed by
Kluwer Law International
P.O. Box 322
3300 AH Dordrecht
The Netherlands

ISBN 90–411–1227–8
Series ISBN 90–411–9670–6

British Library Cataloguing in Publication Data
A catalogue record for this is available from the British Library

Library of Congress Cataloging-in-Publication Data
Conflicting legal cultures in commercial arbitration : old issues
and new trends / Stefan N. Frommel and Barry A.K. Rider (eds.).
p. cm. – – (Studies in comparative corporate and financial law:
v. 4)
ISBN 9041112278. – – ISBN 9041196706 (series)
1. Conflict of laws– –Arbitration and award. 2. Arbitration and
award, International. I. Frommel, Stefan N. II. Rider, Barry
Alexander K. III. Series.
K7690.C66 1999
341.5'22– –dc21

99-35739
CIP

Typeset in 11/13 pt Times by Midland Book Typesetting, Loughborough
Printed and bound in Great Britain by Antony Rowe Limited, Reading, Berkshire

Contents

Preface

The Institute of Advanced Legal Studies has long had more than a passing interest in the resolution of disputes other than through the traditional judicial system. In part this stems from the position of the Institute as *de facto* the law library of the Commonwealth and hence its exposure to and interest in a variety of mechanisms and systems for the resolution or mediation of disputes beyond those contemplated by the English common law. In recent years the Institute's role as the national law library for Britain has necessitated a much greater degree of involvement in legal systems outside the Commonwealth and the traditions of the common law. Consequently, successive Directors of the Institute have encouraged interest in the law and practice relating to alternative dispute resolution procedures. It is in this context that this volume of essays has been assembled and published.

The Institute held a series of public lectures during its jubilee year, on the law of arbitration under the chairmanship and inspiration of Professor Stefan Frommel. The lectures were generously supported by Simmons & Simmons and Kirkland & Ellis and attracted considerable interest. The calibre of speakers and the quality of their papers was such that there was widespread support for the proposal that the Institute should produce a collection of the essays, supplemented by one or two additional contributions. Professor Frommel and I undertook to do this and this volume is the result of, I must say, largely Professor Frommel's powers of persuasion and persistence. The collection is not as disparate as it may at first seem. The theme is the development of arbitration as a device, and the law and practice that has grown up around it, in the context of commercial disputes. Of particular interest, is the essentially cross-cultural perspective of this discussion reflecting, of course, one of the primary strengths of the very process of arbitration. The Institute is in the process of establishing other initiatives and programmes on the basis of this highly successful project and contemplates the drawing together of its work in the area of alternative dispute resolution under a research centre.

The editors wish to acknowledge the considerable support that they have received from the contributors to this book. All are busy scholars and practitioners and all have undertaken revision and up-dating of their papers to render them relevant and accurate at the date of publication. The editors must also acknowledge the assistance of Mr Richard Alexander, The Rowe and Maw Research Officer in European Law, at the Institute for assisting in the co-ordination of the project, as well as, of course, our publishers, Kluwer Law International.

Professor Barry A.K. Rider
Jesus College, Cambridge
1 July 1999

Biographies of Authors

Dr. Christian Borris

Dr. Christian Borris is a specialist in corporate and commercial law and arbitration, educated at the Universities of Giessen and Cologne and the University of Miami School of Law. A Partner in the Cologne office of Deringer Tessin Herrmann & Sedemund, Dr. Borris was admitted as a Rechtsanwalt in 1989 and was further admitted to the Oberlandesgericht of Cologne in 1994. He previously served as Legal Assistant to the President of the Iran–United States Claims Tribunal in the Hague from 1987 to 1989. Dr. Borris is a member of the German Bar Association, the German–American Lawyers' Association and the German Institution of Arbitration.

Bernardo M. Cremades

Dr. Bernardo Cremades holds doctorates in Spanish law, from the University of Seville, and German law, from the University of Cologne. He is a highly distinguished arbitrator, among his many present posts being President of the Spanish Court of Arbitration and of the Arbitration Commission of the High Council of the Spanish Chambers of Commerce, Industry and Navigation, Member of the Chartered Institute of Arbitrators in London, the Panel of Foreign Arbitrators of the London Court of Arbitration, the Court of Maritime Arbitration in Monaco and the International Council for Commercial Arbitration. He has previously held such posts as Associate President of the Arbitration Committee of the United Nations for Perishable Products in Geneva, Chairman of the Arbitration Commission of the World Peace Through Law Center and Member of the Panel on Arbitration of the ICSID. He is also a practising advocate, member of the Bars of Madrid, Paris and Brussels.

Professor Cremades has enjoyed a no less distinguished academic career: *Catedrático* Professor at the University of Madrid and Member of the Academic Council of the International Institute for Business Law.

He has published numerous articles and books, both in Spanish and English, on the subjects of international commercial law and arbitration, among them *Panorámica española del arbitraje comercial internacional*, Madrid 1975; *Arbitraje comercial internacional* (2nd edn.), Madrid 1984, *Litigating in Spain*, Kluwer 1989, *Arbitration in Spain*, Butterworths 1991 and *Business Law in Spain*, Butterworths 1992.

Jonathon Crook

Jonathon Crook is a partner in the Hong Kong office of Simmons & Simmons. He was educated at the University of Cambridge, where he graduated with First Class Honours in Law, and at Yale Law School. He was admitted as a solicitor in England and Wales in 1991 and in Hong Kong in 1995. Prior to joining Simmons & Simmons, Jonathon worked for Standard Chartered Bank in Bombay where he represented the bank in relation to various proceedings, including actions in the Bombay High Court and arbitrations arising out of the Bombay securities scandal of 1991–1992.

Jonathon specialises in commercial litigation and arbitration, contentious insolvency matters and regulatory disputes. He has written a number of articles on arbitration in Hong Kong and the Asia Pacific region.

Horacio A. Grigera Naón

Dr. Horacio A. Grigera Naón is Secretary General of the International Court of Arbitration of the International Chamber of Commerce. He was educated at the University of Buenos Aires and Harvard Law School and holds doctorates from both. Dr. Grigera Naón, a member of the Bars of Buenos Aires, New York and the US Supreme Court, has practised in the field of international business law and international commercial arbitration for some 25 years and has published widely on both of these topics.

Serge Lazareff

Dr. Serge Lazareff, an avocat with Lazareff & Associés in Paris, is a specialist in corporate law and international arbitration. He was educated at the University of Paris and Harvard Law School, where he was a John Harvey Gregory Fellow. Dr. Lazareff has advised the French Government on a number of major projects, in particular during the negotiations surrounding Eurodisney, in which he advised both the French Republic and the Département of Seine-et-Marne. He previously served with NATO, on General Eisenhower's personal staff from 1951 to 1952 and then as Legal Adviser to the Commander-in-Chief of NATO at the Allied Forces Central Europe Headquarters from 1952 to 1967. He has since served as Foreign Trade Adviser to the French Government.

Serge Lazareff was General Counsel for International Operations and Vice President of Asia Pasific of Pechiney, a major French Co-operation.

Dr. Lazareff has enjoyed a prestigious career in arbitration, having appeared either as Chairman, arbitrator or counsel in 70 cases before such tribunals as the International Chamber of Commerce, the London Court of International Arbitration and UNCITRAL. These cases have involved the application of the laws of a wide variety of jurisdictions including France, England & Wales, Greece, Brazil, Korea and several US states. He is Chairman of the International Arbitration Commission (the French National Committee of the ICC), the ICC Working Group on Terms of Reference. He is the chairman of the ICC Institute of World Business Law and of the PIDA programme which is the ICC International Training Programme.

He is also Director of the Mediation and Arbitration Center of the Paris Chamber of Commerce and Member of the ICC International Arbitration Commission.

Andreas F. Lowenfeld

Andreas F. Lowenfeld is Herbert and Rose Rubin Professor of International Law at New York University School of Law, where he specialises in both public and private international law, international economic transactions, litigation and arbitration. He was educated at Harvard University and Harvard Law School. Before joining New York University, he served as Special Assistant, Assistant Legal Adviser and Deputy Legal Adviser to the US Department of State. He is also a member of the Institut de Droit International, has twice been a Lecturer at the Hague Academy of International Law and has served as Associate Reporter for the American Law Institute's *Restatement (Third) of the Foreign Relations Law of the United States*. Professor Lowenfeld has published widely on various aspects of international trade, investment, finance and dispute settlement, including *International Litigation and Arbitration*, *International Economic Law*, a 6 volume series, and, most recently, *International Litigation and the Quest for Reasonableness.*

Ambassador Malcolm Wilkey

Ambassador Malcolm R. Wilkey, a specialist in the areas of international, commercial and administrative law, has been an arbitrator at the highest level since 1991. He served on the United States–Chile Arbitration (Bryan–Suarez) Commission and in arbitration under the US–Canada Free Trade Agreement. Earlier in his career, Ambassador Wilkey held three Presidential appointments in the US Government, rising to Assistant Attorney General of the United States. Following 9 years in private practice, he returned to public service in 1970 as United States Circuit Judge of the US Court of Appeals for the District of Columbia Circuit and finally US Ambassador to Uruguay from 1985 to 1990. He was Chairman of President's Committee on Revision of Federal Ethics Laws in 1989 and Special Counsel to the US Attorney General for the Inquiry into the House Banking Facility in 1992.

Ambassador Wilkey's academic career has been no less notable, including Visiting Chairs at Brigham Young Law School, San Diego Law Summer School in Oxford and Tulane University Law Summer School in Grenoble and membership of the Law Faculty of Wolfson College, Cambridge. He has published widely, including *Is It Time For A Second Constitutional Convention?* An attorney admitted to the Bars of Texas, New York, the District of Columbia, the US Supreme Court and the Second, Fifth and Ninth US Circuit Courts of the District of Columbia, Ambassador Wilkey was also Adviser on the Restatement of the Foreign Relations Law of the US for the American Law Institute and is a Fellow of the American Bar Foundation.

Sigvard Jarvin

Sigvard Jarvin is a member of the Paris and the Swedish bars. He was general counsel to the ICC International Court of Arbitration, Paris (1982–1987) and member of the Court (1988–1995). He is in charge of Lagerlöf & Leman's Paris office, is engaged in international business practice with an emphasis on international arbitration and head of Linklaters & Alliance International Arbitration Group in Paris. Mr. Jarvin is the author of *Guide to Arbitration and Related Services offered by the ICC* and co-author of *Commercial Arbitration Law in Asia and the Pacific* and of *Collection of ICC Arbitral Awards.* He is general editor of the *Stockholm Arbitration Report* and responsible for the arbitration chronicle in *Lamy Contrats Internationaux.*

Jean Reed Haynes
Jean Reed Haynes is a partner in the New York office of Kirkland & Ellis. She practises in the areas of international and domestic arbitration and as a commercial trial lawyer. She was assisted in preparation of this paper by Leigh Hyer, an associate in the Washington, DC office of Kirkland & Ellis, and Sara Mogulescu, an associate in the New York office of Kirkland & Ellis.

1

The Reconciliation of Conflicts Between Common Law and Civil Law Principles in the Arbitration Process

Dr. Christian Borris

I. THE ISSUE

1. Introduction

On being asked to contribute to this work, I was informed that its overall theme was: 'How arbitration can, in a civilised manner, resolve the differences that arise between parties coming from different legal cultures.' Such a title clearly assumes that there is a universal understanding of 'civilised manners'. Although I do not seek to question this assumption *per se*, arbitration, as a procedural concept, is in itself an expression of manners, namely, the manner of settling legal disputes. Consequently, dealing with differences in procedural rules means dealing with differences in 'manners'. Further, an absolute standard of civilised manners simply does not exist and the mere fact that a given set of manners is different from one's own should not automatically (dis)qualify them as 'uncivilised'. A better overall theme might therefore perhaps have been, 'How arbitration can manage the different civilised manners of parties coming from different legal cultures'.

At least as far as the settlement of commercial disputes is concerned, the differences in legal culture between the common law and civil law appear to relate to the procedure by which results are arrived at rather than to the results themselves. In probably the majority of all cases, the outcome of the proceedings would be the same whether conducted in a civil law or common law court. This does not mean, however, that in an

Conflicting Legal Cultures in Commercial Arbitration, S. Frommel and B. Rider (eds), Kluwer Law International, London, 1999; ISBN 90-411-1227-8

international dispute the choice of forum is irrelevant. The procedural rules applicable in national courts are (normally) designed primarily to settle domestic disputes, i.e. disputes between nationals of a particular country. The proceedings are conducted in the official language of the court; the judges are nationals of the country in question and have been educated in its legal tradition. For these reasons, a party is almost always at a natural disadvantage in proceedings before a national court of another jurisdiction. Such disadvantages can, however, be avoided in arbitration.

It is often the experience of the legal adviser in contractual matters that the parties have different philosophies with respect to clauses regulating the settlement of disputes. Some are simply not prepared to consider arbitration as a means of settling disputes because they feel uncomfortable with the fact that the arbitral tribunal's decision cannot be appealed or because the duration and cost of arbitration proceedings are seen as disadvantages. Such parties believe that litigation in a national court is in any event preferable to arbitration and are prepared to accept the jurisdiction of a foreign court. They know, of course, that they will have to live with the peculiarities of the foreign court's rules, that they will have no choice but to retain the services of legal counsel admitted to such court and that the proceedings will be conducted in the official language of the country where the court is situated.

Others accept arbitration, not only as the lesser evil but as a distinct preference. There are a number of reasons for this. Firstly, because they feel that to submit to the jurisdiction of a national court in the country where the other party is located would give that other party an advantage. Submission to the jurisdiction of the national courts of a third country is hardly ever appropriate, quite apart from the risk that the courts of that third country may not accept jurisdiction over the case. Arbitration is the only alternative. Secondly, arbitration is often preferred because it allows the parties to select arbitrators with specific expertise required for a particular dispute. Confidentiality is another appreciated feature of arbitration. Finally, arbitration is often faster and less costly than proceedings before the national courts, particularly where those proceedings go to several levels of appeal.

Parties who opt for arbitration as the means of settling their legal disputes expect the arbitration proceedings to be conducted in a manner which is fair to both parties, without strict adherence to the procedural rules applicable in the national courts of the country in which they take place, or indeed any particular set rules other than those expressly agreed to.

2. The Principle of Party Autonomy

Most modern arbitration laws enacted in the last one or two decades recognise the contracting parties' desire for procedural flexibility and generally leave vast room for party autonomy in this respect. Mandatory provisions and interference with the arbitral proceedings by state courts are reduced to a minimum. This is true, for example, of the UNCITRAL Model Law on International Commercial Arbitration which has been adopted by a large number of countries.[1] It is also true of the new English Arbitration Act 1996, which incorporates most of the provisions of the UNCITRAL Model Law. The Report of the Departmental Advisory Committee on Arbitration Law expressly states that '... one of the main purposes of the [Act] ... is to encourage arbitral tribunals not slavishly to follow court or other set procedures'.

3. Procedural Discretion of the Arbitral Tribunal

Whilst modern arbitration legislation is almost unanimous in its attempt to reduce mandatory provisions to a minimum (usually to provisions guaranteeing equal treatment of the parties and the right to be heard), there is a growing tendency to offer the parties a more comprehensive set of procedural rules rather than leaving the conduct of the proceedings completely to the discretion of the arbitral tribunal.[2] Predictability of the conduct of the proceedings is, of course, an important element in the strengthening of the parties' confidence in this means of dispute settlement and we know that for this reason parties often prefer to agree upon the rules of an arbitration institution such as the ICC Rules, LCIA Rules,

[1] Germany has adopted the UNCITRAL Model Law with effect as of 1 January 1998.

[2] This is, for example, the approach of the UNCITRAL Model Law. Under the new Swiss Arbitration Act 1989, on the other hand, the procedure, in the absence of any agreement between the parties, is largely left to the discretion of the arbitral tribunal.

UNCITRAL Arbitration Rules or German Institution of Arbitration Rules, to name just a few. Such rules then replace the vacuum which may be left by national legislation or other rules applicable in the absence of a contrary agreement between the parties.

Neither the non-mandatory rules applicable in a particular jurisdiction nor the procedural rules of arbitration institutions adopted by parties by agreement, however, offer answers to all the procedural questions that may arise in an international commercial arbitration. On the contrary, such laws and regulations are normally deliberately phrased in such a way as not to prejudice the arbitral tribunal's discretion, for example with respect to the issues to be addressed. Rather, it is the task and art of the arbitral tribunal to fill the gaps left by arbitration laws and institutional arbitration rules.

Attempts have been made to develop some sort of guidelines for handling procedural problems in arbitration proceedings involving parties from different legal cultures. In 1983 the International Bar Association promulgated the Supplementary Rules Governing the Presentation and Reception of Evidence in International Commercial Arbitration. These may be particularly helpful to those parties preferring to follow detailed pre-set rules for certain aspects of the taking of evidence in international commercial arbitration. The UNCITRAL Notes on Organizing Arbitral Proceedings, published in 1996, are also very useful. These describe the various procedural approaches and solutions available to arbitral tribunals in a given case without, however, expressing any particular preference.

In order to ensure that both parties accept the way in which the arbitral proceedings are conducted, procedural rules should preferably be agreed upon by the parties themselves. In this context, the arbitrators should use their skills to assist the parties to reach agreement. If agreement cannot be reached the arbitral tribunal will have to use the discretion left to it either by legislation or by institutional arbitration rules. The arbitral tribunal should, in exercising the discretion granted to it, adopt rules which are fair to both parties and which allow the proceedings to be as efficient as possible, given the particular circumstances of each case.

'Fair to both parties' means that the procedural rules adopted should offer both parties an equal opportunity to present their argument. Such rules should not take either party by surprise nor particularly favour one party. In international commercial arbitration, the set of rules should be such that neither party is required to retain the assistance of foreign local lawyers in order to be sure of avoiding formal or procedural mistakes.

Anything else would clearly frustrate the expectations of the parties to the arbitration agreement.

While fairness is the most important aspect, the second test to which procedural rules should be subject is 'efficiency'. In international commercial arbitration, more than in other types of litigation, the parties are commercial companies and business people for whom one of the reasons for choosing arbitration is the desire for a quick decision. Procedures or rituals that may historically have developed in the practice of the national courts, but which lead to delay, should therefore not be followed in arbitration.

It is useful to start by describing and analysing some basic distinguishing features between procedural rules in the common law and civil law systems. In doing so in a simple manner, generalisations are inevitable. There are significant national variations within each of the two systems and they are often more subtle than presented here.

II. THE ORIGIN OF DIFFERENCES BETWEEN COMMON AND CIVIL LAW PROCEDURE

It is common ground to state that it is the purpose of procedural rules in both legal traditions to ensure a 'fair trial' and 'due process'. Equal treatment of the parties, as well as the right and opportunity to be heard before the court, are also universally accepted principles. Differences can be found, however, in the implementation of these principles. In order to examine if, and to what extent, procedural rules peculiar to the one or the other system should or should not be followed in international commercial arbitration, it is helpful to analyse the origin of such peculiarities.

Some of the peculiarities of common law procedure appears to result from the fact that the history of democracy in England is older than in most civil law countries. Similarly, mistrust of state authority is more indigenous in England than in many civil law countries. This was one of the reasons for introducing the jury trial, i.e. a trial in which the court is assisted by a jury composed of laymen.[3] Although in England – in contrast

[3] See, e.g., Smith and Bailey, *The Modern English Legal System* (2nd edn., 1991) at 706 quoting Atkin LJ in *Ford* v. *Blurton* (1922, 38 TLR 801 at 805): [The jury is] 'the bulwark of liberty, the shield of the poor from the rich and the powerful.'

to the US[4] – jury trials in civil cases are now the rare exception,[4/5] the rules of procedure, as they have historically developed, remain somewhat oriented towards the concept of a jury trial.[6] Courts in civil law countries, on the other hand, are regularly composed of state-employed, professional judges without a 'jury'.

The jury tradition may be the origin of another characteristic distinction between common law and civil law procedure: the common law 'adversarial' approach versus the civil law 'inquisitorial' maxim. The adversarial approach is characterised by a passive role of the judge, whereas the judge in the inquisitorial civil law systems is not only permitted but expected to take a more active role in the conduct of the proceedings.[7] A passive judicial role is obviously more appropriate in a system in which the final decision is taken by a jury rather than the judge himself.

In considering the ways in which the existing differences between legal cultures can be reconciled, it is important to bear in mind the origin of those differences. This may be illustrated by discussing some of the distinguishing features of the respective procedural laws.

III. CONFLICT OF PROCEDURAL PRINCIPLES AND THEIR RECONCILIATION

1. Written Pleadings / Oral Hearing / Role of the Judge

Common law procedure is typically oriented towards the oral hearing. The written pleadings exchanged prior to the oral hearing mainly serve as preparation for it and are not necessarily expected to be excessively detailed. For example, documents or exhibits are not attached to such pleadings.[8]

4 In the US, the jury was also regarded as providing protection against English judges. See Schack, *Einführung in das US-amerikanische Zivilprozeßrecht* (1988) at 55; Heidenberger, 'Der amerikanische Jury-Proze*ß* in Produkthaftungsfällen' in (1982) *RIW* at 872.

5 Smith and Bailey, *op. cit.*, at 703.

6 This is probably even more true in the US, where jury trials in civil cases are more frequent.

7 For a more detailed discussion of the adversarial and inquisitorial approaches, see Borris, 'Common Law and Civil Law: Fundamental Differences and their Impact on Arbitration' in (May 1994) *Arbitration* 78 *et seq.*

8 See, e.g., Patocchi and Ian L. Meakin, 'Procedure and the Taking of Evidence in International Commercial Arbitration' in (1996) *RDAI/IBLJ* 7 at 885.

All details of the case deemed relevant by the parties must be pleaded at the oral hearing even if such pleadings have already been made in the written statements. Witness examinations may well be 'rehearsed' prior to the trial with the assistance of a party and its counsel. Consequently, the common law hearing, which has been described as 'a major theatrical performance',[9] may last several weeks, which is virtually unknown in civil law procedure.

The concentration of the proceedings on the oral hearing would appear to result from the fact that traditionally, the case had to be prepared for a jury trial. The jury is not involved in the proceedings prior to the oral hearing. It decides the facts of the case solely on the evidence presented at the trial. It is therefore necessary to restate fully at the oral hearing all evidence relating to the facts of the case.

In civil law procedure, the parties are required to state their case with all necessary, in some instances even excessive, detail and to present, or at least identify, all documents and evidence relied on as early as possible in the proceedings. In German civil procedure, for example, a statement made or evidence offered by the party may, under certain circumstances, be ignored if the court finds that it could and should have been presented earlier in the proceedings and that its late consideration now would delay the proceedings.[10]

Generally, the common law judge takes a passive role in the proceedings, for example leaving the examination of witnesses to the parties or their counsel, and does not, on his own initiative, encourage the parties to settle the case or even make any specific proposal to assist them to do so.[11]

In contrast, the civil law judge typically takes a more active role, examining witnesses himself. It is generally considered unethical for a party's legal representative to influence in any way a witness or his testimony before the court. A rehearsal of witness statements is regarded as completely inappropriate.

The judge in the civil law system is more likely actively to encourage the parties to settle the case. For example, § 279 German Code of Civil Procedure explicitly provides:

[9] Patocchi and Meakin, *op. cit.*, p. 885.
[10] § 296 German Code of Civil Procedure.
[11] See below.

> The court shall encourage an amicable settlement of the dispute or of parts of the dispute at each stage of the proceedings.

This in turn is considered unethical in the common law system.

In international commercial arbitration, there is no compelling reason why the parties should not be obliged to disclose all facts and legal arguments, together with all documentary and other evidence on which they intend to rely, as early as possible in their written pleadings prior to the hearing.[12] Consequently, the purpose of the oral hearing can be limited to the clarification of any remaining questions and the examination of witnesses and experts. Considering that

(i) the majority of disputes in international commercial arbitration are of a technical and complicated nature,
(ii) the arbitral tribunal is composed exclusively of legal or other experts and professionals who, at the hearing, are fully familiar with the contents of the file,
(iii) no jury is involved in the proceedings,

there is no need to repeat at the hearing the contents of the written pleadings. Both the opposing party and the tribunal are in a position to study the arguments and evidence submitted thoroughly and quietly. The tactic of surprise at the oral hearing will, in contrast, often cause avoidable and undesirable delay.

Moreover, there is nothing wrong with the arbitral tribunal taking a more active role in the conduct of the proceedings, in particular at the oral hearing. This will serve to focus the proceedings on those issues which are in dispute and will foster efficiency. At the same time, more interaction between the parties and the arbitral tribunal will make the process of reaching the decision more transparent for the parties and help them to identify their position. Far from being inappropriate it is indeed desirable that the arbitral tribunal conducts the decision-making process in a transparent fashion, provided, of course, that it is careful not to create the impression of being prejudiced by its own (preliminary) statements in the proceedings.

Even the common law lawyer not used to such an active role on the

[12] This seems to have become the favoured approach and prevailing practice in international commercial arbitration; see Craig, Park and Paulsson, *International Chamber of Commerce Arbitration* (2nd edn., 1990) chapter 24.01.

part of the arbitrator will not be put at a disadvantage. If it is correct that the passive role of the judge in common law tradition stems from the fact that historically the judge left the actual decision to the jury, and was not to influence the jury's decision by his conduct of the proceedings, this will not be a valid concern in arbitration, where there is no jury to be convinced.[13]

Whether the arbitral tribunal should, on its own initiative, encourage an amicable settlement between the parties poses a more difficult question. The possibility cannot be ignored that an arbitral tribunal may feel, if not legally, certainly psychologically bound in an award not to deviate too far from an amicable settlement that it had previously proposed but which was not accepted by one or both parties. Nevertheless, it would not appear inappropriate for the arbitral tribunal to carefully explore whether the parties are prepared to settle the case without going through the entire arbitration process. A specific proposal for a settlement, however, should only be made upon the request of both parties. In any event, it should be reasoned. It should identify the areas of uncertainty with respect to legal and factual issues. Where the proceedings have reached a stage at which an expert has to be appointed to determine relevant facts, the tribunal may consider proposing that, in view of the complexity of the matter, the delay, costs and uncertain outcome of an expert opinion, it might be in their interest to reach a settlement. In contrast, however, it would not normally be appropriate for the tribunal to make a proposal 'out of the blue' unless expressly requested by both parties to do so. To do otherwise would almost certainly leave the parties with the impression that their arguments had not been carefully considered by the arbitral tribunal and that the tribunal may not be prepared to come to a completely different decision, even having considered these arguments.

In any event, parties from civil law jurisdictions should take into consideration that an arbitral tribunal composed of arbitrators educated

[13] Even in the English national courts, judges are permitted to take a more active role in civil and commercial cases. Cf. Smith and Baily, *op. cit.,* at 707: In a civil action it may prove difficult for a judge to refrain from intervening with questions and observations. However, the judge does not have to attain the standards of objectivity and neutrality as opportune in a criminial trial, since usually no jury is present. The procedure is relatively flexible in a civil trial and the absence of the jury enables the judge to take a more positive line over matters which may be considered to be irrelevant or uncontentious. However, the judge must not take such an active part in the case that it appears that counsel is deprived of the conduct of the action.

in the common law system will generally be more careful in making proposals for an amicable settlement than civil lawyers may be used to from their own court practice. For his part, the common law arbitrator should realise that lawyers from civil law jurisdictions often hesitate to approach the other party in order to explore the possibility of settling the case until the court has expressly encouraged the parties to do so. This is a situation in which the arbitral tribunal must prove its skill in helping the parties settle their case without creating the impression of being prejudiced.[14]

2. Pre-Trial Discovery

Pre-trial discovery describes a process preceding the oral hearing by which each party is entitled to 'discover' evidence which is not available to it. Typically, pre-trial discovery encompasses the right to request the production of documents in the possession of the other party which are, or are believed to be, relevant to the case, as well as the statements of witnesses (so-called depositions). In the common law tradition, pre-trial discovery is regarded as one of the most important means of ascertaining the truth.[15]

In contrast, the civil law jurisdictions are not familiar with a procedure comparable to pre-trial discovery in this sense. Here, a party's right to request the production of documents in the possession of another party is very limited; such rights are usually regarded as existing under substantive law rather than procedural rules. Although pre-trial discovery procedures do differ to some extent in the various common law jurisdictions,[16] they are generally vigorously rejected by many lawyers in civil law countries, mainly for the reason that these procedures create the risk of an inappropriate invasion of privacy and 'fishing expeditions'. As far as Germany is concerned these fears appear to result from experiences of

[14] Section 12 of the UNCITRAL Notes on Organizing Arbitral Proceedings makes a pragmatic proposal: 'Given the divergence of practices in this regard, the arbitral tribunal should only suggest settlement negotiations with caution. However, it may be opportune for the arbitral tribunal to schedule the proceedings in a way that might facilitate the continuation or initiation of settlement negotiations.'

[15] Mustill and Boyd, *Commercial Arbitration* (2nd edn., 1989) at 324; Patocchi and Meakin, *op. cit.*, at 891; Borris, *op. cit.*, n. 7 at 82.

[16] For pre-trial discovery in the US, cf. Borris, 'Die Internationale Handelsschiedsgerichtsbarkeit in den USA' in (Cologne 1987), *Rz.* at 227–236.

American lawyers attempting to conduct full-scale pre-trial discoveries in German companies, involving dozens of lawyers invading the offices of the company and searching for documents.[17]

Pre-trial discovery seems to be particularly important in a system in which there is a strict separation of the oral trial and the proceedings which precede it, as is the case under the common law. If the parties are not obliged (or at least not to the same extent as in the civil law system) to disclose the facts and evidence upon which they rely as early as possible in the proceedings, but can rather wait until the oral hearing itself, it is only fair to give each party the opportunity to compel the other party to disclose it. In contrast, in the civil law system, the facts and evidence are presented by the parties more gradually in the written pleadings leading to the oral hearing. It is in the interests of both parties to submit all relevant evidence as early as possible in order to avoid the risk of the facts or evidence not being admitted at a later stage in the proceedings. This renders the discovery of documents to some extent unnecessary.

Of course, pre-trial discovery goes further than that; it gives a party the right to request the production of documents in the possession of another party which the other party would not necessarily wish to disclose in the proceedings.[18] There would not appear to be anything wrong with this, provided that the request for disclosure of a given document serves only to establish facts relevant to the particular case. Problems may arise, however, when a party is forced to produce a large number of documents which may not be relevant.

In this context it should be noted that under many modern arbitration statutes, the arbitral tribunal is given the discretion to order discovery measures, but is not obliged to do so. The option existing under the old English Arbitration Act 1950 to request a discovery order from the High Court has been abandoned. Moreover, an application to annul an arbitral award merely on the basis that the arbitral tribunal refused to order discovery has, on occasion, been refused by the English High Court (for example in a decision of 1981).[19] Discovery procedures are not frequently ordered in arbitration, and, when they are ordered, are restrictive in their application. Apart from the fact that these procedures are often not accepted by parties who are not from common law countries, discovery

17 Cf. Weigand, 'Discovery in der internationalen Schiedsgerichtsbarkeit' in (1992) *RIW* at 361 *et seq.*

18 See, e.g., Smith and Bailey, *op. cit.*, at 559.

19 'The Anangel Peace' (1981), 1 Lloyd's Rep. 452, 454.

orders may be difficult or impossible to enforce in many civil law jurisdictions. Although in principle the Hague Convention of 18 March 1970 on the Taking of Evidence Abroad in Civil or Commercial Matters does not exclude judicial assistance with respect to pre-trial discovery measures, even in arbitral proceedings, Germany, for example, has made an express reservation to the effect that it will not grant judicial assistance in relation to orders for the disclosure of documents. Should the tribunal order or permit pre-trial discovery measures which are not complied with voluntarily by one of the parties and which cannot be enforced, the arbitral tribunal will have no other way of sanctioning this conduct of a party than by drawing negative conclusions from the fact that a party is not prepared to disclose the documents in question. If, and to what extent, it will be permitted to do so without violating public policy may not always be clear in a given case, and the arbitral tribunal should not conduct the proceedings in such a way as to jeopardise the recognition and enforceability of the arbitral award.

Depositions of witnesses are generally regarded more favourably in civil law countries. From a civil lawyer's point of view, depositions basically fall within the category of examination of witnesses. The only difference is that the examination of the witness takes place in the absence of the arbitral tribunal and under the control of the parties. Although, from the civil lawyer's perspective, such a procedure outside the control of the tribunal creates the risk of a witness being unduly influenced, it may contribute to establishing at an early stage in the proceedings whether the witness (or party) can clarify the issues. Depositions may thus help to focus the proceedings. They may also be particularly helpful in international commercial arbitration where witnesses are not able or willing to appear in person before the arbitral tribunal.[20]

Discovery procedures should thus not be categorically rejected in international commercial arbitration. First, discovery should be permitted to the extent that both parties agree voluntarily to co-operate in the discovery process. In the absence of agreement, however, discovery should only be ordered in restricted circumstances.[21] This is particularly true for the discovery of documents.[22] Depositions of witnesses or parties may be

[20] See Craig *et al.*, *op. cit.*, chapter 26.

[21] Cf. Craig *et al.*, *op. cit.*, chapter 26.01.

[22] Art. 4(4) of the IBA Supplementary Rules attempts to restrict discovery of documents as follows:

A party may ... request any other party to provide him with any document

permitted, but the questions asked of the deponent should, in essence, be defined in advance. Considering that parties from civil law jurisdictions would generally not expect to be subjected to discovery procedures, the arbitral tribunal should generally be careful in drawing negative conclusions from such party's refusal to produce documents.[23] This may be justified, however, where the refusal to produce a specific document, identified by the other party, is not supported by a valid reason, or where, under the applicable substantive law, one party is entitled to request the production of documents on other legal grounds.

3. Cross-Examination

In common law countries, cross-examination, i.e. the examination of witnesses by both parties rather than the judge, is believed to be the best method of testing the credibility of a witness. Due to the fact that first the party presenting the witness is entitled to ask questions of the witness (examination in-chief), followed by questions from the other party (cross-examination), combined with the requirement to re-state all relevant facts of the case at the oral hearing, the examination of witnesses in common law procedure normally takes considerably more time than under civil law.

In civil law procedure, it is usual only to examine witnesses with respect to contentious issues. Moreover, witnesses are primarily examined by the judge and only thereafter by the parties' counsel. Thus, the examination of witnesses is focused on statements deemed relevant by the judge, and although the parties would normally be given the opportunity to ask questions themselves, such party-conducted examination would rarely extend to the cross-examination of the common law tradition.

cont.
relevant to the dispute between the parties ..., provided such document is identified with reasonable particularity and provided further that it passed to or from such other party from or to a third party who is not a party to the arbitration.

[23] Art. 4(6) of the IBA Supplementary Rules, however, expressly states that 'if a party fails to comply with the Arbitrator's order to produce any relevant document ..., the Arbitrator shall draw his conclusions from such failure'; cf. also Craig *et al.*, *op. cit.*, chapter 8.09; Patocchi and Meakin, *op. cit.*, at 892; Borris, 'Die UNCITRAL-Schiedsregeln in der Praxis des Iran–United States Claims Tribunal' in *Jahrbuch für die Praxis der Schiedsgerichtsbarkeit*, Band 2 (1988), p. 3, 16; INA Corporation and Government of Islamic Republic of Iran, Award No. 184-161-1 (13 Aug. 1985), 8 Iran–U.S.C.T.R. 373, 382.

With respect to the method of examining witnesses, the common law and civil law approaches can be easily combined in arbitral proceedings. The examination of witnesses by the tribunal and by the parties directly are not mutually exclusive. Both methods can, and should, be used in international commercial arbitration in a supplementary way. A party should not be denied the opportunity of asking questions directly of a witness or expert. In which order questions are asked in a particular case may depend on the circumstances and should be agreed between the arbitral tribunal and the parties. Thus, whether the tribunal asks questions first and then gives the parties the opportunity to ask questions, or *vice versa*, can be decided on a case-by-case basis.[24]

Cross-examination in the classical common law sense, however, should generally not be practised in international commercial arbitration where one party comes from a civil law country.[25] It is peculiar to the common law system and, in fact, an 'art' with which civil law parties are not familiar. The fact that the rehearsal of witness statements[26] preceding the oral hearing is regarded as unethical practice in the civil law tradition is an important reason for not compelling a party to do this simply to avoid being placed at a disadvantage in the proceedings.[27] While it is perfectly acceptable for critical questions to be asked of a witness by the parties as well as by the tribunal, it is not necessary in arbitration to stage witness examinations in the form of theatrical performances. In contrast to

24 Art. 5(9) of the IBA Supplementary Rules takes a more definite approach: 'Any witness who gives oral evidence shall in the first place be questioned by the Arbitrator and thereafter submit to examination by the party calling him, cross-examination by all other parties and re-examination by the party calling him.'

25 See Craig *et al.*, *op. cit.*, chapter 24.01: 'Such tedious practices are largely unkown in ICC arbitration ...'

26 Such rehearsal should be distinguished, however, from 'interviewing' a witness in order for a party to find out whether a witness can indeed testify with respect to particular questions of fact. Accordingly art. 5(8) of the IBA Supplementary Rules states: 'It shall be proper for a Party or his legal advisers to interview witnesses or potential witnesses.' Of course, the nature and extent of such 'interviews' may vary. It is therefore prudent for the arbitral tribunal, as proposed in para. 67 of the UNCITRAL Notes on Organizing Arbitral Proceedings, in order to avoid misunderstanding, to clarify what kind of contacts a party is permitted to have with a witness in the preparation for the hearings.

27 See Borris, *op. cit.*, n. 7 at p. 80.

'interviews', the rehearsal of witness examinations should thus be discouraged in arbitration. The examination and cross-examination of witnesses should be focused and strictly limited to disputed issues. Cross-examination in this sense is not only acceptable, but also of considerable use in international arbitration.

4. Parties as Witnesses

Another distinction between common law and civil law procedure is the issue of whether a party's statement is admissible in the proceedings as 'evidence'. In other words, can a party be a witness?

The common law tradition generally accepts that a party may give evidence as a witness, while civil law jurisdictions generally do not, or at least only in exceptional circumstances.[28] It is worth noting in this context that German law, for example, treats the so-called organs of a legal entity, e.g. the managing directors of a limited liability company, who by statute are its representatives, as a 'party', even though the actual party is the legal entity which they represent. The civil law systems are reluctant to accept parties as witnesses for two basic reasons. Firstly, it is considered unlikely that the testimony of a party called as a witness will differ from the stand already adopted in the papers that have been submitted in their capacity as a party to the proceedings. Secondly, under German law, for example, a party heard as a witness is liable to severe criminal penalties if their oral statement proves not to be true and correct. The law simply wishes to avoid the party being faced with a conflict of interest.

The question whether a party's statement may be introduced to the proceedings as evidence is almost invariably purely academic. The arbitral tribunal would normally not prevent a party from making any statements in the proceedings in support of its own case. Whether such statements have the formal status of 'evidence' is rarely decisive for the outcome of the case, considering that the arbitral tribunal has vast discretion in weighing and assessing the 'evidence' offered in the light of the parties' own submissions. The arbitral tribunal will not, of course, ignore the fact that the party 'witness' has a personal interest in the outcome of the case. A party should be permitted, therefore, to make any statements they wish. However, they should not be put under oath, nor should they be required to leave the meeting room during the proceedings. This has been the

[28] See Borris, *op. cit.*, n. 7 at 81.

practice, for example, of the Iran–United States Claims Tribunal at The Hague. In such cases, the minutes of the proceedings would normally state:

> Mr. X provided the Tribunal with information without making the declaration required of a witness.[29]

With such a pragmatic approach, there is no need to come to a final conclusion as to whether witness statements are to be defined as 'evidence' or simply the parties' submissions.

5. Written Witness Statements

Written statements of witnesses are generally not accepted as evidence in civil law procedure. There are, however, exceptions to this rule, for example in preliminary summary proceedings.

In contrast, common law systems generally do accept written witness statements and treat them as evidence, subject however, to each party's right to request cross-examination of a witness.

Since written witness statements are prepared on the initiative and under the control of one party, their evidentiary value may sometimes be questionable. Often, however, they help to give a more comprehensive picture of the relevant facts at the stage of written pleadings. Each party knows on what evidence their opponent is relying and in some cases the other party may decide that it will no longer dispute certain facts when they realise that their opponent is in a position to produce witnesses in their support.[30]

Moreover, written witness statements, like depositions, are particularly helpful in international commercial arbitration involving parties from different and often distant countries, and also where it is difficult, if not impossible, to subpoena a witness to appear before the arbitral tribunal. Experience shows that witnesses who decline to travel to appear before

29 See Borris, *op. cit.,* n. 23 at 16.

30 Cf. Lörcher, 'Improving Procedures for Oral and Written Witness Testimony', ICCA Congress Series No. 7, XIIth International Arbitration Congress Vienna, 3–6 November 1994, Planning Efficient Arbitration Proceedings. *The Law Applicable in International Arbitration* 145 at 148, 149; para. 61 of the UNCITRAL Notes on Organizing Arbitral Proceedings; Craig, Park and Paulsson, *op. cit.*, chapter 24.05.

an arbitral tribunal may well be prepared to submit a written witness statement.

The arbitral tribunal should never refuse, however, to examine a witness *in personam* if this is requested by one party, provided that the testimony of such a witness could be material. If handled in this way, written witness statements may be a useful instrument in arbitration. It is difficult how this could prejudice a party from one or the other legal culture.

6. Expert Witnesses

In common law procedure, expert witnesses are either appointed by the parties or, upon the application of either party, the court may appoint an independent expert.[31]

In the civil law system, the independent expert is almost always appointed by the court. Although the parties are free to obtain the opinion of an expert and to produce his opinion in the proceedings, such opinion would be treated as the submission of a party rather than 'evidence'. Therefore, in order to avoid unnecessary costs, expert opinions are rarely obtained by the parties except where they may further substantiate and clarify a party's submission and lend it additional credibility. If, however, the other party disputes the accuracy of the opinion, the judge would nearly always appoint an independent expert.

It appears that the issue is of a purely academic nature. In practice, expert opinions are obtained and introduced into the proceedings by both the arbitral tribunal and the parties, depending on the circumstances of the case. Arbitral tribunals in international commercial arbitration normally pragmatically avoid an explicit decision as to whether a party-introduced expert opinion is to be regarded as 'evidence' or a party statement. As the arbitral tribunal has complete discretion in weighing evidence, whether or not expert opinions constitute actual evidence or simply a party's submission will not normally have an impact on the outcome of the case. Accordingly, the conflict between procedural principles in this case can be avoided simply by leaving the issue open.

[31] Cf. Patocchi and Meakin, *op. cit.*, at 885. The new English Arbitration Act 1996 explicitly permits the arbitral tribunal to appoint an expert on its own initiative.

IV. CONCLUSION

It may be seen from these examples that modern arbitration law and practice offer many instruments with which conflicts between different legal cultures in arbitration proceedings can be managed in a 'civilised manner'. In fact, international commercial arbitration procedures accomplish that which is not even attempted by the national courts. A party submitting to the jurisdiction of a foreign court cannot expect that court to make allowance for the fact that one party may not be familiar with the particularities of the applicable rules. This will not necessarily place the foreign party at a disadvantage, but it may do, starting with the fact that the proceedings are conducted in a foreign language. This is not to say that recourse to the national courts, even a foreign court, is always the worse solution. It is clear, however, that parties in international commerce are more frequently choosing arbitration as their preferred means of settling disputes, and they do so because they feel that a truly international forum is more neutral than a national court.

Hence, it is the arbitral tribunal's duty not to frustrate the parties' expectations when agreeing to an arbitration clause and to conduct the proceedings on the basis of rules which may fairly be regarded as common ground for both parties. There is no categoric answer as to how best to do this in a particular case. The best tailor-made solution always depends upon the circumstances of the case, the parties involved and the mentality of the arbitrators. Arbitration offers all the flexibility, procedural techniques and instruments that are needed for this purpose. Both the arbitral tribunal and the parties should make full use of these to ensure fair and efficient proceedings.

2

International Arbitration as Omelette: What Goes into the Mix

Andreas F. Lowenfeld

I.

My title is meant to be humorous, but not cynical. Indeed my thesis – and my experience – is that gradually – that is over at least the quarter century that I have observed the process first hand – the mix has been improved. On the whole the better features of the contributing legal systems have been poured into the mix, and the less attractive features have been strained out.

This is not to suggest that international arbitration is an ideal system, or even, to paraphrase what Churchill said about democracy, that it is the worst system of dispute settlement except for all the others. I think it works fairly well because most of the participants – parties, counsel, and decision-makers – have, or come to have, a common understanding of the process.

I do not want to overstate the conclusion. I did have one losing counsel in a case where I was sole arbitrator call me to say, 'I think the result was wrong, you misinterpreted the contract, but you were always fair, you had a correct understanding of the parties' legitimate needs, your rulings on evidence and discovery were sound, and neither I nor my client have any quarrel with the process'. That kind of message makes an arbitrator feel good. I had another case where I presided over a three-person panel, in which the chairman of the losing party – a mid-sized American corporation in a dispute with its European distributor – sent me a long hand-written letter that started out 'Arbitration sucks, and you, Professor, most of all'. The language got worse, but the sentiment remained the same.

Conflicting Legal Cultures in Commercial Arbitration, S. Frommel and B. Rider (eds.), Kluwer Law International, London, 1999; ISBN 90-411-1227-8

The controversy – not an uncommon one – arose when the American manufacturer saw its European sales decline, and attributed the decline to failure of the distributor to use his best efforts to push the manufacturer's product. That part of the controversy – alleged breach of the distributorship contract was clearly subject to an agreement to arbitrate, pursuant to the Rules of the International Chamber of Commerce. When the manufacturer filed suit in a US District Court, the distributor had no difficulty in obtaining a stay from the court and an order to arbitrate. But the manufacturer's claim went further: 'Not only', said the manufacturer, 'is the distributor not pushing our product, he is pushing his own product, which infringes our patent'. That claim was not a contract claim, and not subject to the agreement to arbitrate. Thus when the counsel met with the arbitrators to fix the terms of reference, every paragraph contained a clause saying '. . . without prejudice to the action pending in the District Court concerning validity and infringement of US Patent No. 000000'.

Thereafter, and prior to the plenary hearing, counsel for the two sides apparently said to themselves and to each other, 'The two proceedings, one in court and one in arbitration, will involve the same parties, much of the evidence will be the same, and the arbitrators seem level-headed and ready to go, while we may have to wait years to get the patent case heard in court'. (Also, they may have thought that whoever prevailed in the arbitration would have difficulty in enforcing an award with another action between the same parties still pending.) So counsel jointly wrote to the arbitrators asking whether they could submit the patent controversy to us as well. The arbitrators, fortified by a recent amendment to the US patent law, that for the first time permitted arbitration of patent disputes,[1] said 'Fine'. Amended terms of reference were prepared incorporating a submission agreement drawn up by the parties with the arbitrators' assistance, and a hearing was arranged encompassing all aspects of the dispute. I thought the process went well, with some cross-pollination between members of the patent bar and the commercial litigators, as well as between the one patent lawyer on the panel and the other two who knew about arbitration but not much about patents. At the end of the hearings counsel for both sides thanked the tribunal and said that they had saved not only several years but a good deal of money by submitting the entire dispute to us.

That, of course, was before the decision, and reflected the view of the lawyers. All the more regrettable, I thought, to receive the letter from the

[1] 35 U.S. Code §294, adopted in 1982.

client, who – putting aside his intemperate words – must have thought 'What a fool I was to have listened to the lawyers and agree to arbitrate the entire dispute'. I am sure he told his staff, 'Never again.'

I tell this story because there is a tendency, when members of the arbitration community get together, to pat themselves and each other on the back. On the whole, my paper does so too. Some grains of salt belong in the omelette as well.

II.

I am often asked, by lawyers drawing up contracts, as well as by students, what body of rules or institutions should be selected in an agreement to arbitrate. My answer, which surprises many people, is that it makes very little difference once the arbitration is under way. Arbitration rules and administering institutions are important in connection with deposits, fees, selection of arbitrators, and in theory – but I think only in theory – for the time taken by the process.[2] The ICC rules have the unique features that the arbitrators' award is scrutinized by the Court of Arbitration (which is actually a committee, not a court) before it may be issued.[3] But once the arbitration is under way, there are no real rules, or to be more accurate, it is the arbitrators – usually but not always with the consent of counsel – who make the rules. I have served as arbitrator in cases conducted under rules of the ICC, ECE, UNCITRAL, SMA, AAA, (domestic and international) Stockholm Chamber of Commerce, and *ad hoc* proceedings without any reference to rules, and while each case is different, the differences depend on the nature of the controversy, the skill and background of counsel, and the experience and disposition of the arbitrators, not on the rules provided for in the agreement to arbitrate.

The drafters and frequent users of rules know this, and also understand that if they attempted to draw up real rules of procedure, analogous for instance to the rules of practice contained in the English Rules of Practice, the American Federal Rules of Civil Procedure, or the German ZPO, they

[2] For a convenient comparison, provision by provision, of the UNCITRAL, ICC, and AAA rules, see Susan W. Tiefenbrun, 'A Comparison of International Arbitral Rules' in (1992) 15 *Boston College Int'l & Comp. L. Rev.* 25.

[3] International Chamber of Commerce, Rules of Arbitration, art. 21. See also, W.L. Craig, W.W. Park, and J. Paulsson, *International Chamber of Commerce Arbitration*, Ch. 20 (3rd edn., 1998).

would be negotiating forever and negotiating in the abstract. And so the ICC rules say in Article 15 (1998 version):

> The proceedings before the Arbitral Tribunal shall be governed by these Rules, and, where these Rules are silent, [which on many issues is likely to be the case] by any rules which the parties or, failing them, the Arbitral Tribunal may settle on, ...

The LCIA rules say, in Article 5:

> The parties may agree on the arbitral procedures and are encouraged to do so.
>
> In the absence of procedural rules agreed by the parties or contained herein, the Tribunal shall have the widest discretion allowed under such law as may be applicable to ensure the just, expeditious, economical, and final determination of the dispute....

The American Arbitration Association International Arbitration Rules say, in Article 16:

> Subject to these rules, the tribunal may conduct the arbitration in whatever manner it considers appropriate, provided that the parties are treated with equality and that each party has the right to be heard and is given a fair opportunity to present its case.

And so on.[4]

III.

What then do arbitrators do with all their freedom? Is it really like the story told in my traditional, strict high school about its sister school

[4] No parallel statement appears in the UNCITRAL Arbitration Rules. But practice under those rules, and particularly arts. 24–26, in effect also leaves the conduct of the proceedings – written and oral – up to the arbitrators, unless the parties have made their own agreement, for instance with regard to discovery or use of translators, or in agreements such as the Algiers Accords establishing the Iran–US Claims Tribunal or the North American Free Trade Agreement, (NAFTA), which incorporate the UNCITRAL Rules by reference.

dedicated to progressive education, where little Johnny asks 'Teacher, do we have to do as we please today?' I don't think so.

In the first place, experienced arbitrators will issue some procedural guidelines at the beginning of the proceeding, whether in a meeting to fix the terms of reference or other pre-hearing conference, or in a written order. Such an order will not resolve all issues that come up in the course of an arbitration, and indeed some points may have to be reconsidered. But a skilful arbitrator tries to settle as many procedural issues as possible before they become contentious, and before a breakdown in consensus becomes apparent.

I am not sure if my own experience provides a large enough sample to draw a persuasive inference. In the 1970s, however, I participated in a number of arbitrations in which the arbitrators, coming from different cultures and legal systems, had significant differences about the conduct of the arbitration. Should parties, as contrasted with witnesses be permitted to testify? Should requests for documents be made to the arbitrators and screened by them before being transmitted to the adverse party, or should such requests be exchanged directly between the parties? Should questioning of witnesses be conducted by the arbitrators, on analogy to continental judges, or by counsel? Should cross-examination be permitted, and if so when?

The outcome – in individual cases and in a group of cases over, say, a five-year period – was more like a salad than an omelette, with individual inputs depending on where the arbitrators and counsel came from – what they were used to in their court systems.

In the interim, it seems to me that the arbitrators and counsel have become more experienced with international arbitration and have drawn on those experiences more than on their home country's legal systems. I cannot remember a serious disagreement with a fellow arbitrator about the conduct of an arbitration in the past ten years. The closest I came was with a chairman who issued an order of procedure calling for a three-hour lunch break. We had a large number of witnesses scheduled, and I did not think a three-hour lunch – even when consistent with the habits at the *situs* – was either an efficient use of time or conducive of alertness when the hearings would resume at four o'clock. But as to the role of the tribunal in questioning the witnesses, production of documents, deadlines for various steps, simultaneous or consecutive submissions, and so on, there were no disagreements at all.

IV.

What then is this growing consensus about how to resolve commercial disputes across national frontiers? Is there a kind of *lex mercatoria* for arbitral procedure? I think so, though I prefer to avoid that term which has become too controversial for my purposes here.[5]

First, it is clear that the Anglo-American tradition in favour of oral hearings is now firmly established. When the UNCITRAL Rules were being put together in the mid-1970s, that was not obvious, and Article 25 of those rules begins 'In the event of an oral hearing ...'. Ten years later, the drafters of the UNCITRAL Model Law assume that there will be a hearing – 'unless the parties have agreed [otherwise]' – an agreement I have never seen. And while hearings may be split – say phase I on liability and phase II (if necessary) on damages, or phase I on liability and compensatory damages, phase II (if appropriate) on consequential damages, or phase I on issues of law, phase II on the evidence – the Model is clearly a sustained consecutive period in which parties, counsel, and arbitrators are focused on the dispute before them, as in an English or American trial, not as a continental civil proceeding. Of course in part the concentrated hearing is a product of the need to schedule parties, counsel, witnesses, and arbitrators. But I think it also reflects the shared perception that what matters most are the facts, and that a concentrated hearing with live testimony is the best way to establish the facts.

Even assuming agreement on holding a hearing, it was for a long time not clear whether there would be cross-examination, English-style. The European model would have the judge do the questioning, with the lawyers making suggestions or filling in at the end, and some arbitrators modelled their role on that of the judge in their home country. I have seen American counsel surprised and shocked that they were not expected to conduct the examination of their witnesses and the cross-examination of those of their opponents.

I think by now, however, the value of cross-examination as the best way to get at the truth and to resolve conflicts of evidence has become generally accepted in international arbitration. I believe this is a good development. It is all right for arbitrators to ask questions when a point

[5] For my views on *Lex Mercatoria generally*, see A. Lowenfeld, 'Lex Mercatoria: An Arbitrator's View' in Thomas E. Carbonneau (ed.) *Lex Mercatoria and Arbitration*, Ch. 3 (1990), also published in (1990) 6 *Arbitration International* 133.

is not clear – which often happens when witnesses (and I include parties) address a subject to which they have devoted their professional careers but which is quite alien to the arbitrators. What do I know about oil drilling, washing machines, electric power generators, or the intricacies of counter-trade? But the kind of questioning that tests a witness' veracity by going from proposition A to B to C and finally back to 'then A is not as you said it was' seems to me unseemly for an arbitrator, and especially a party-appointed arbitrator. Even if the arbitrator is prepared to treat witnesses for both sides in the same fashion, such questioning may well raise doubts, justified or not, about the arbitrator's neutrality. Moreover, I find that even when I have read all the documents and briefs beforehand (which is not always the case), I cannot be as well prepared on the facts and issues as counsel, who has an incentive to master the facts and who more frequently is supported by a team to help him or her do so. I am persuaded that cross-examination should be done by counsel, and I believe this is now very largely agreed. Indeed I think the practice is becoming contagious, so that it is gradually catching on in European courts as well.

When a well-prepared lawyer conducts the cross-examination, it is not only good theatre, it often serves to confirm or resolve doubts. Of course not all lawyers are skilled at cross-examination: the kind of questioning that takes the form of 'Mr. Witness, did you say X?' 'Yes.' 'On what do you base that ...?' may just give the witness a chance to make a damaging point clearer than it was on direct examination. My impression is that continental and Latin American counsel are gradually becoming more familiar with cross-examination, and learning to do it better. That also means that the lawyers are learning to put more emphasis and preparation on evidence, as contrasted with the legal doctrine. That too, I think, is a sound development.

If I have described a trend moving international arbitration toward the Anglo-American model, I think that is not accidental. By and large the common law tradition of trials is a better model than the civil law tradition, particularly before decision-makers who are not career officials like the European judges, but are drawn from law practice or academic careers for a particular controversy.

But the common law model, and particularly the American version, has its downside. The rules of evidence, for instance, which were developed to guard against misleading a jury or protecting an accused person from the powerful police and prosecutor, do not make much sense in commercial disputes before professional jurists. In my experience these rules play very little role in international arbitration. Hearsay is not excluded, and generally not even pointed out. It seems perfectly natural if the witness is asked 'How did you find out about X?' for the witness to say 'Mr. M. told me'. The next question is 'What did M tell you?' and perhaps 'Did M tell you how he found out?'

I have no doubt that arbitrators can sort out how reliable such information is, and where it fits into a larger picture that emerges. Objections would be overruled, and if they were made too often, resented.

Documents are routinely accepted, even if only a photocopy is tendered. I did have an episode recently – the first in my experience – in which a document tendered by one side as an official government decree was challenged by the side representing the government as a forgery. The arbitrators did not know quite how to handle this, and we eventually found a formula in which we said the claim in question did not turn on that document anyway. I was not wholly satisfied with the outcome, because if the document really was a forgery – i.e., a signature, a government stamp, and the text of a draft put together in a montage and then photocopied – that would have cast doubt over much of the submission of the party that tendered it – the 13th stroke of the clock discrediting not only itself but the 12 that came before. On the other hand, if the document was genuine, a false accusation of forgery would severely impair the credibility of the party making the accusation. But deciding such a question on the basis of an artificial burden of proof – unconvincing in court – would I think be regarded as out of place in arbitration.

That brings me to my last item, the one that most divides not common law from civil law, but American practice from the practice of the rest of the world. I am referring of course to discovery, the favourite indoor sport of American lawyers, and the *bête-noire* of all others who must deal with them.

Here, I think, a genuine compromise has been reached, though nowhere clearly articulated. Of course the idea that Americans sue first, then rummage through their opponents' files to build their case – which is in any event overdrawn[6] – could not work in a trans-cultural setting. Such

[6] Compare, for example, the following statement by Lord Diplock in *British Airways Board* v. *Laker Airways Ltd.* [1984] 3 WLR 413 at 419, [1984] All ER 39 at 44, [1985] AC 58 at 78, in which the House of Lords nevertheless reverses the Court of Appeal and discharges an injunction that had prevented Laker from continuing its antitrust action against British Airways in the United States:

discovery is also usually not necessary in arbitration, even in the eyes of American lawyers. The parties to an international arbitration know one another, and nearly always are both in possession of most of the relevant documents. 'Sue first, then investigate' may be necessary for the patient who was wheeled unconscious into the operating room and does not know who was the surgeon, who the anaesthetist, and so on.[7] Wide-ranging discovery requests, beginning with 'All memoranda, minutes and correspondence ...' are usually not necessary in commercial arbitration, and are needlessly burdensome. On the other hand, the statement in both the AAA International Rules and the UNCITRAL Rules that 'each party shall have the burden of proving the facts relied on to support its claims or defence'[8] should not lead to the inference a party cannot secure material documents from the other side.

I cannot remember an arbitration in which there were not some disputes about discovery. But in general parties or their counsel understand that they are obligated to turn over specific documents requested by the other side.

cont.

My Lords, one of the characteristics of the rules of civil procedure in the federal courts of the United States (as well as in most state courts), which seems to any English lawyer strange and, indeed, oppressive upon defendants, is that a 'complaint', the document by which an action is begun, while it alleges that the complainant has a cause of action against the defendant or defendants, does not disclose, or discloses only in a most exiguous form, the facts which the plaintiff will eventually rely upon at the trial as giving rise to that cause of action. Instead, the complaint is accompanied, or immediately followed, by a request to the defendants for pre-trial discovery which bears little resemblance to the kind of discovery that is available in English civil actions. Its breadth, the variety of methods, oral and written, that it makes available for a wide-roving search for any information that might be helpful to the case of the party seeking discovery, the enormous expense, irrecoverable in any award of costs to a successful defendant, in which it may involve parties from whom discovery is sought, and its potentiality for oppressive use by plaintiffs, particularly in antitrust actions, receive sufficient mention in the various speeches in this House in *In re Westinghouse Electric Corporation Uranium Contract Litigation* [1978] AC 547. What for present purposes is important particularly as respects the civil action by [British Caledonian] is that if the American action ever reaches the stage of trial, what evidence in support of its complaint Laker will by that time have unearthed by the process of pre-trial discovery it is as yet impossible to foretell;...

7 Even in England, discovery before suit is permitted in such cases. See Rules of the Supreme Court O.24, r. 7A; Supreme Court Act 1981 ss. 33(2), 34(2).

8 See AAA International Arbitration Rules, as Amended and Effective 1 April 1997, art. 19(1); UNCITRAL Rules, art. 24(1).

What if they don't do so? Some arbitrators are prepared to issue orders, though they have no bailiff to enforce them. Others prefer to indicate that failure of a party to comply with a reasonable document request will be held against it – not only in determining a specific fact against the non-producing party but more generally in assessing the good faith of that party. My experience is that such 'indications' – arbitrators do not like the word 'threat' – usually have the desired effect.

The most difficult issues of discovery concern requests for documents – or testimony – of former employees of a party and assertions that particular documents contain confidential proprietary information. The requesting party never believes that the ex-employee is no longer under control of its adversary, and often the arbitrators do not believe it either but feel constrained to refrain from expressing their doubts. It is generally understood that in international arbitration one cannot get discovery from third parties, at least reluctant ones; treating the ex-employee – especially if he or she 'retired' after the arbitration was begun – as a third party witness puts a strain on the process not easy to manage.

The assertion of trade-sensitive information is equally difficult. I am sitting on a case right now in which A says B stole its invention, and modified its trademark slightly, in violation both of the law and of the contract between them. B says it improved the product and secured its own patent. A demands B's design drawings for the purpose of showing that B 'reverse-engineered' A's product. B says we cannot give our designs to A, our bitterest competitor.

It is difficult to sort out this issue, which may well be crucial to the outcome of the case. We thought of a protective order, but B asks that disclosure be limited to A's lawyers, and A's lawyers reply that they need the known-how of A's technical people. Anyhow, B asks, how can the protective order be policed?

I do not know how this issue will be resolved. My point for present purposes, however, is that it will not be determined on the basis of the law of A or the law of B or the law of the chairman's home state. Three arbitrators, who did not know each other previously but who have all had experience with international arbitration, will draw on that experience and will work out a solution. The solution will not be 'law' in the sense that one can find it in a rule or statute book, but I am almost certain that it will reflect a consensus among the three of us, and if we handle it right will be accepted by both sides. I would add – without here opening up a whole separate subject – that I expect that the party-appointed arbitrators will address the puzzle not from the point of view of which solution favours the side that appointed them, but which solution seems most conducive to a just and expeditious resolution of the overall dispute.[9]

V.

Finally, how can you find out about what I have said, to corroborate, confirm, controvert, or prepare for? I recently had a call from a lawyer in California whom I did not know – a friend of a friend – who had heard that I knew about international arbitration. This lawyer, an experienced litigator, had inherited a large international arbitration – i.e., there was a sizeable amount of money at stake – and he asked if I would be available for a consultation.

The first question he put to me when he came to my office was 'How can I stop this arbitration – can I get an injunction?' The answer was pretty easy: the contract in dispute contained an ICC arbitration clause which had no apparent defects, so that it would be a waste of time to try to enjoin the arbitration, and could only annoy the arbitrator who had already been appointed. But the question puzzled me: Why was this lawyer so anxious to avoid arbitration? Well, it turned out primarily because he did not know what to expect. He assumed that he could get no discovery. 'Not so,' I said. Well, could he get the kind of discovery he was used to under the Federal Rules of Civil Procedure? Probably not, unless he made an agreement with his adversary, who was also an American lawyer, but to try to do so, I said, would be a big mistake. Whom could he call as witnesses? What about depositions? ... cross-examination, rules of evidence, protective orders, appeal?

At the end of our three-hour session, my new friend was somewhat relieved, but still felt that he was about to swim in a pool whose depth he did not know. He would not know what requests or proposals to put before the arbitrators and when to object to the requests of his adversary.

[9] Note that I use the terms 'party-appointed' or 'party-nominated' and 'presiding arbitrator' or 'chairman,' but not 'party arbitrator' for the former or 'neutral arbitrator' for the latter, because in my submission all arbitrators are supposed to be neutral, and in my experience most in fact are. For more on this topic, see A. Lowenfeld, 'The Party-Appointed Arbitrator in International Controversies: Some Reflections' in (1995) 30 *Texas Int'l Law J.* 59, reprinted in (November 1996) 11 *Mealey's Int'l Arbitration Report* 1.

He asked if I would sign up as counsel and accompany him to the hearings. I would have liked to do it. Even as I have learned a good deal about advocacy from being an arbitrator, I would have learned more about arbitrating from serving as counsel or co-counsel.

In the actual case, it turned out that I was unable to take the assignment. But the episode led me to think whether, without putting out a major treatise or undertaking a monumental project such as the ICC's Uniform Customs and Practice for Documentary Credits, there would be a way to widen the circle of participants in the institution of international arbitration as I have described it.

Perhaps I have a conflict of interest, in that there is a kind of club of participants in international arbitration, and I seem to have become a member. But I am a teacher first – not a missionary but a teacher – and I have a desire to pass on what I have learned.

The process of arriving at something like a procedural consensus has come about as arbitrators and counsel from one country or system have come together with arbitrators and counsel from other countries and other systems, have learned from and taught their new colleagues, and have spread their learning and experiences rather like a game of Liaisons Dangereuses. Counsel in one case become arbitrators in another, and *vice versa*. Party-appointed arbitrators become chairmen, nominees of institutions are chosen by parties, and so on. I suspect that an attempt to codify all this learning and experience, so that everyone could pull out a little red book, as French lawyers do, or a big White Book, as British lawyers do, would be misleading, unless every paragraph began with 'Unless otherwise agreed ...' or 'Subject to the discretion of the Tribunal ...' Still, something could perhaps be done to make newcomers to the field feel more welcome – perhaps some kind of manual or handbook, not another sermon for the converted, but something to instill confidence in my new friend who is off to Paris without me. I think that one can do better than the paraphrase from Humpty Dumpty that reads 'The Tribunal may conduct the arbitration in whatever manner it considers appropriate'.

To come back to my original metaphor, everyone knows that you can't make an omelette without breaking eggs. But if it is too much to ask for a cookbook full of recipes, it may not be too much to hope for a detailed – and user-friendly – description of the permissible ingredients.

3

International Arbitration: Towards a Common Procedural Approach

Serge Lazareff

The unification of procedural methods has become a subject *à la mode*. Indeed, the practitioner of international arbitration no longer accepts the basic distinction which prevailed only a few years ago: common law proceedings on the one hand, civil law proceedings on the other hand.[1] Whatever the forces responsible for blurring the dividing line between these traditional choices, we can only note amongst arbitrators and practitioners alike the increasing awareness of an emerging 'harmonised procedural pattern' in international arbitration.[2]

This common procedural approach has already been presented favourably as one which has the good sense to combine the best elements of both legal systems while avoiding their pitfalls.[3] This portrayal is further illustrated by examples noted below of the areas where harmonisation seems to have been achieved.

However, certain reservations exist. For instance, there remains at least one serious lingering difference between common law lawyers and those of the civil law which should be highlighted in order that lessons be drawn from it. This is their attitude towards witnesses.

Finally, the comment has been made that while arbitration practice is

1 See Robert Briner, 'Domestic Arbitration Practice in Continental Europe and its Lessons for Arbitration in England' in (1997) 13 *Arbitration International* 155; see also Marcel Storme 'International Arbitration – A Comparative Essay' in (1994) *European Review of Private Law* 359.

2 Sir Michael Kerr, 'Concord and Conflict in International Arbitration' in (1997) 13 *Arbitration International* 121.

3 Kerr, *op. cit.* at 126. I therefore will dispense with developing examples which have been already so remarkably well presented.

Conflicting Legal Cultures in Commercial Arbitration, S. Frommel and B. Rider (eds), Kluwer Law International, London, 1999; ISBN 90-411-1227-8

indeed evolving in the direction of a common procedural approach, at present no uniformity exists whatsoever.[4] While this is an accurate observation, we should not be striving for uniformity, but rather flexibility. In certain situations, the conduct of common law style proceedings is, and should remain, a viable option regardless of the fact that procedural methods overall appear to be 'Continentalising'[5] in international arbitration.

I.

My discussion begins with England, for England is also the mother of commercial arbitration. The English, or rather London, tradition in this field dates from time immemorial. London did not produce the dichotomies which the followers of the French approach to arbitration were, and still are, so familiar with: national versus international arbitration, or the distinction based on the civil or commercial nature of the dispute. London arbitration traditionally dealt with disputes arising in connection with a standard form of contract subject to English law, regardless of whether the transaction was domestic or international.

In France, the rule was originally against arbitration in domestic matters, except those related to commerce. Surprisingly for a country which has made so much progress in arbitration, there are still some very restrictive provisions in the Civil Code. One such provision prevents the state and the *collectivités territoriales* (i.e. the region, *département*, etc.), from going to arbitration in internal matters, although they may do so, in certain cases, in international trade matters. Using the negotiation of the Disney agreement, that is, the Convention between the French authorities and Disney for the setting up of the park near Paris as an example will better explain the difficulties involved.

The counsel to the French government and to the county of Seine and Marne wanted to include in the Convention an arbitration provision, but could not do so, because of the general prohibition of the Civil Code, without first obtaining the enactment of a specific law. This special Act of Parliament required some lobbying and the matter first went all the

4 Robert Briner, *op. cit.* at 159.
5 Marcel Storme, *op. cit.* at 369.

way up to the Prime Minister. Finally, the law was voted and was inserted in a finance law.[6]

Fortunately, in France, arbitration has become quite popular. There is even support from the courts: when the former President of *Cour de Cassation*, the highest French court, was appointed, he was asked his position on arbitration. 'Arbitration, arbitration, arbitration', he responded, 'for two reasons: the first, what you do we don't have to do; the second, in many fields you are more professional than we are'.

The distinction between domestic and international arbitration, as mentioned above, does not exist in England, or at least has not until very recently. The English approach is specific in other respects, the finding of facts comes particularly to mind because the English approach is very different from the French. The importance which the English attach to the facts may be most readily seen by the French observer in the fact-finding role reserved to the jury. Behind this organisation, there is an attachment to fact-finding which the French would qualify as obsessional: the English (and the Americans) believe that there exists *a* truth, *the* truth, and the facts therefore must be painstakingly reconstructed to show it.

The French approach could not be more different from the English. The French judge, or arbitrator for that matter, will not go looking for the truth *per se* because his jurisdiction is strictly limited to the contentions brought immediately before him by the parties in their pleadings. Within this written framework created by the parties, the French judge or arbitrator will decide a case almost exclusively on the basis of the parties' written arguments and those documents which they have chosen to submit.

What this shows is the simple fact that, in the background, there remain, on either side of the Channel, fundamental differences in outlook. This observation however should not prevent one from recognising that a common approach has nevertheless thankfully, been forged in many domains.

One of the most remarkable examples of harmonisation may be found in the complete agreement which prevails concerning the autonomy of the arbitration provision. Much ground has, indeed, been covered since Judge Lagergren rendered a very famous award in 1963 in which he refused to look at the case because it seemed to him that bribery had been used to obtain the agreement.

[6] Arts. 2060 and 2061 of the French Civil Code.

The author once sat on an arbitral tribunal which also had to deal with the issue of bribery. An award was rendered which can be discussed because it was published. The decision of the arbitral tribunal was that the allegation of bribery did not prevent the tribunal from looking at the facts of the case because there was an arbitration provision which had to be enforced. The defendant challenged the jurisdiction of the tribunal before the Swiss Federal Tribunal, which ruled in favour of the tribunal's jurisdiction. Nothing is left of Lagergren's position whereby the arbitrator could not touch a case involving corruption. It is, to use the words of the tribunal, *dépassé*. Thirty years of evolution in the field of international arbitration have instead imposed upon the arbitrator the duty to go into the case and examine the contract. It is precisely his mission.

This trend towards harmonisation finds further support in the severability of the arbitration provision. As an illustration, there was recently a case between the State of Iran and a corporation from another country. The problem which arose involved article 55 of the Iranian Constitution which states that an arbitration provision must be approved by a decree of the Iranian Council of State. The arbitral tribunal decided that, in an international arbitration procedure, article 55 could not have priority over an arbitration provision which the parties had willingly entered into.

Another example of harmonisation is that of *Kompetenz-Kompetenz*. This principle according to which the arbitral tribunal is sole judge of its own jurisdiction is now universally recognised, for example, in section 30 of the English Arbitration Act of 1996.

Greater harmonisation may also be seen with respect to arbitrability. The *Mitsubishi* case, in which the US Supreme Court decided that arbitrators could hear anti-trust cases, is now well known. In Switzerland, the Federal Tribunal decided that arbitrators may nullify a contract on the basis of articles 85 and 86 of the Treaty of Rome. While they are not empowered to give injunctions, arbitrators may apply the provisions of the Treaty of Rome in order to determine the validity of an agreement. The application by the arbitrator of international law may appear to some to be narrower than the principle underlying the *Mitsubishi* case and so, in this area, the Continent, may be lagging behind common law countries.

The next point involves the Terms of Reference. Under the International Chamber of Commerce Rules, the Terms of Reference are the document in which the arbitrator sets the framework of the dispute. This gives the national courts a yardstick for measuring whether the arbitral tribunal has remained within its jurisdiction. The Terms of Reference also leads quite frequently to settlements since it gives the parties a better understanding of their opponent's case at the outset.

In spite of its clear advantages, the Terms of Reference were subjected to resistance on the part of common lawyers who considered it a waste of time to draft this document. The reticence of its detractors has subsequently waned so that today, in the author's experience, the Terms of Reference are considered commonplace among practitioners, whatever the name of the instrument (Agreement to Arbitrate; Arbitration Protocol, etc.).

II.

In summary, all of the above examples give additional weight to the notion that international arbitration is indeed moving towards a common procedural approach. On the other hand, I must now play Devil's advocate by highlighting what one might call a limiting factor to this evolution.

It has been previously mentioned that a basically written procedure prevails in France and the Continent in general. The result is that the arbitrators will hear a few witnesses if the parties so insist, but if the lawyers speak for more than an hour at the final oral presentation, the arbitrators may become rather nervous. The Continental attitude is the following: 'Don't take one hour and a half, or two hours, we already have the file and know the case.'

The author once sat on an arbitration where the lawyers on both sides, Americans, requested six weeks to hear 60 witnesses. The chairman granted only two weeks, which may come as a surprise to common lawyers. But in the author's experience there has never been a single ICC case where the award was set aside because the time given to counsel had been limited, or the number of exchanges of briefs restricted. It remains, nevertheless, a fact, and this example is intended to show, that the English and the American are more inclined to rely on the testimony of witnesses than their sceptical Continental colleagues who are more apt to rely on contemporaneous documentary evidence.[7] This difference in underlying attitude explains why total harmonisation cannot be achieved by simply instituting a unified set of procedures.

This is also shown by the trend towards harmonisation which may be

[7] Briner, *op. cit.* at 163.

seen in the current practice of asking witnesses to produce statements. It is indeed extremely rare in international arbitration today for a witness not to submit an affidavit to the tribunal before the hearing.[8] These witness statements do not, however, carry the same meaning, or bear the same value, depending upon the legal culture of the arbitrator. Neither is better than the other, but there is a striking difference. Common lawyers, particularly the Americans, will tend to give credence to whatever is signed, particularly if it is sworn. Continental arbitrators, on the other hand, will tend to have little faith in a document which they assume was prepared by someone other than the signatory, that is, the lawyers. In this case, the witness statement alone will be practically of no significance.

Therefore, if there is to be witness testimony, Continental arbitrators will generally wish to see the witness face to face to judge for themselves whether he is credible. Such an appreciation may not be easy following the meticulous preparation which is often given to witnesses. The difficulties caused by their advance preparation, along with the suspicion of inherent bias of a party's non-technical fact witnesses, will thus often lead Continental arbitrators to assign little credit to these witnesses once they have testified.[9]

It is necessary, therefore, to be pragmatic when measuring the significance of the harmonisation which has undeniably taken place. Recognising the extent to which certain things now appear to be done in the same ways must not be allowed to obscure the fact that, on the inside, certain things continue to be perceived quite differently. Our own legal cultures remain, for the time being, in certain areas, an important limiting factor to harmonisation because, as has been shown, the application of the same rule may lead, despite all good intentions, to strikingly different results.

The author's own viewpoint is neither to argue for or against the evolution towards a common procedural approach in international arbitration. It is a simple fact that harmonisation has fortunately occurred in many areas, some examples of which are given above. It has also been shown how differing legal cultures, may, in any event, circumvent harmonised procedures whose significance should therefore not be overestimated.

[8] Kerr, *op. cit.* at 126.

[9] A party's technical fact, or expert witness, on the other hand, is often considered to be more independent by Continental arbitrators.

Whether arbitrators and practitioners, for one reason or another, should endeavour towards a common procedural approach which would be prescribed in all arbitrations is another question, and one to which the answer is 'no'. Complete uniformity is not desirable because flexibility is in fact an essential quality of international arbitration worth defending. The procedural flexibility inherent to arbitration proceedings under many national laws and rules of arbitration constitutes, in practice, not only a means of implementing harmonised procedures in a growing number of cases, but also a way of departing from such procedures when it appears to the parties, or the arbitrators, to be preferable to do so.

An interesting factor is that of the language of the arbitration. Frequently the presence of American (or British) lawyers in a procedure normally leads to the de facto use of US (or English) procedures. Similarly, an American attorney, for example, would not object to applying Continental procedures in a French-speaking case.

Consequently, practitioners today are called upon to exercise flexibility by not going before an international arbitral tribunal as they would before their national judge to try a case. They instead should be prepared to proceed according to the methods of the emerging 'international disputology' to use the words of Michael Kerr. If they are not ready to do so, they run the risk of gaining a reputation for not knowing what international arbitration is all about.

Arbitrators, on the other hand, and practitioners as well, must exercise flexibility by departing from these harmonised procedures when they believe it is appropriate to do so in a given arbitration. The choice should be left entirely up to them within, of course, the limitations of the applicable law and exercised by the arbitrators with fairness and impartiality while ensuring that each party has a reasonable opportunity to present its case. Under article 16 of the French New Code of Civil procedure, the judge must, under all circumstances, apply, and see to it that others apply, the principle that each party has the right to be heard. This should be, as indeed it has become, a universal principle.

Therefore, while it is true that procedural methods tend in general to favour the Continental approach, common law style proceedings are not likely to become extinct in international arbitration so long as they respond particularly well to the needs of certain arbitrations. For instance, one might hear 45 witnesses in a case involving the construction of a nuclear power plant, but not in a matter concerning a minor commercial transaction! If the amount in dispute is sufficiently great, the arbitrators may even decide that the luxury of discovery is available to the parties. The decision of what procedure to follow should never be assumed, but taken on a case by case basis.

4

Leading Arbitration Seats – A (mostly European) Comparative View

Sigvard Jarvin

I. INTRODUCTION

International arbitration offers the advantage – amongst others – over judicial proceedings of allowing parties a greater choice of forum. The parties are not limited to the other party's place of residence, or the place where that party has assets, as they normally are in litigation, but are free to agree on practically any place that suits them to hold the arbitration. The parties' wider scope of choice is due to the existence of a number of conventions which make enforcement of arbitration awards easier to obtain abroad than court judgments.

Where the parties agree on a place of arbitration in an international dispute, this does not necessarily determine the choice of procedural rules. The procedural rules are determined by (i) applicable provisions in the arbitration rules chosen by the parties to govern disputes (institutional or *ad hoc* rules); (ii) a specific agreement between the parties before or after the arbitration has started; (iii) a choice made by the arbitrator by virtue of the applicable rules of arbitration (e.g. in the Terms of Reference or in a separate ruling).

This does not mean, however, that the arbitration is 'denationalised'.

The different concepts of procedural and substantive law in different countries may cause some surprise to the unwary when choosing the place of arbitration. This is what the parties learnt in one case, concerning the

Conflicting Legal Cultures in Commercial Arbitration, S. Frommel and B. Rider (eds), Kluwer Law International, London, 1999; ISBN 90-411-1227-8

question of the statute of limitation.[1] The claimant asserted that Finnish substantive law applied and that there is no statute of limitation in Finnish law. The arbitrator applied the rules of *lex fori*, which stipulated that limitation is a matter of procedure and not of substance. Since he was sitting in England, the application of *lex fori* on the issue was mandatory and the arbitrator came to the conclusion that the claim was statute barred under English law and dismissed the case.[2] The choice of place of arbitration decided the outcome of the case.

II. PARTIES' CHOICE OF THE PLACE OF ARBITRATION

The parties may choose the place of arbitration in the business agreement or when a dispute has arisen. Or they may leave it to be made on their behalf by an arbitral institution or by the arbitral tribunal itself. At some stage, a choice must be made.

Where should an international arbitration be held? Should it be in Amsterdam, Cairo, Geneva, Kuala Lumpur, London, New York, Paris, Stockholm, Vancouver, or Vienna (to name a few possibilities)? There are practical considerations to be made, such as availability of suitable hearing rooms, accommodations, secretarial assistance, communications and other infrastructure. It is also important to note that a rapid development has taken place in many countries in recent years; legislation and practice have changed to respond to the demands of international arbitration. But not everywhere. In some places the international movement towards accepting arbitration is still viewed with hesitation, if not suspicion. As a result, great variations exist with respect to what matters are arbitrable, what form must be given to an arbitration agreement, the degree of judicial intervention in the arbitration process, the means of challenging an arbitrator, the freedom of choice of the law applicable to the merits, whether several arbitrations may be joined together into one single proceeding, whether discovery is possible, what conservatory measures are available, etc.

1 Extracts of the award have been published and commented by Sigvard Jarvin in (1985) 2 *Journal of International Arbitration* 1 at 75.

2 The English law has since changed. Under the Foreign Limitation Periods Act 1984, where a foreign law applies, the rules of that foreign law relating to limitation should apply.

The parties to an international commercial arbitration are thus generally free to choose the place of arbitration. This is true for most arbitration systems.[3]

An example showing how the parties have used this freedom is the so-called US/USSR Optional Clause Agreement (1977) which provides that arbitration shall take place in Stockholm, Sweden.[4] The said agreement is intended for inclusion in contracts between legal or natural persons of the US and the former foreign trade organisations of the USSR. It is a good example of a modern trend in commercial arbitration: the choice of a 'neutral' place of arbitration.

By making the choice themselves, the parties are well-positioned to take into account various parameters that are important for the smooth and efficient running of the arbitration. One such factor is the cost of arbitration, the availability of foreign exchange and the freedom to transfer it. A second factor is the time and the costs of travelling. By choosing a place of arbitration in a third country, both parties to the contract will have the inconvenience of travelling and staying abroad; neither of the parties is therefore favoured at the expense of the other. A third factor for the parties to consider is the availability of law reports and law books on both *lex causae* and *lex fori*; where the choice of either of these laws has been made in the parties' contract, they can fix the place of arbitration in the country where access to the books and reports is easy. But where there is no agreement, and since the place of arbitration must be fixed before the arbitrators have decided the choice of *lex causae* and *lex fori*, it is convenient to fix the place of arbitration in a neutral country where international arbitration is accepted and developed; the chances of obtaining access to the necessary material and expert legal advice is thereby enhanced.

To site the place of arbitration in the defendant's country is not without risks. In contracts with powerful organisations, mostly state-owned, often in developing countries, who have had a strong bargaining position in their contract negotiations with a private firm, it is not unusual to find the place of arbitration fixed by contract in the country of the state organisation. Often in cases where the local party has been the defendant,

3 See for example, the UNCITRAL Arbitral Rules, art. 16. However, arbitration under the ICSID rules takes place in Washington and the approval of the Secretary-General of the ICSID and the arbitrators must be obtained if the arbitration is to be held elsewhere.

4 Published in *Arbitration in Sweden* (2nd edn., 1984) Stockholm at 205.

it has used all kinds of procedures and devices to stop the arbitration from going forward. These may include efforts to exercise influence on local and national authorities in order to obtain refusal by competent authorities to issue visas to the arbitrators or the opposing party's counsel, court litigation against the other party and injunctions against the arbitrator.

III. REDUCING THE IMPORTANCE OF THE PLACE OF ARBITRATION THROUGH INTERNATIONAL CONVENTIONS AND OTHER INITIATIVES

In view of the progress in international commercial arbitration through the late 1970s and early 1980s, the United Nations considered that it would be helpful to offer a model on international arbitration legislation. One useful purpose, at least, would be served if a majority of countries adopted similar legislation, namely the importance of the choice of the place of arbitration would be reduced, since many local differences relating to the arbitration procedure would have disappeared.

On 21 June 1985, the United Nations Commission on International Trade Law (UNCITRAL) adopted a Model Law on International Commercial Arbitration. The Model Law is intended to serve as a model of domestic arbitration legislation, harmonising and making more uniform the practice and procedure of international commercial arbitration while freeing international arbitration from the parochial law of any given adopting state. Its existence should be of particular value not only in countries which would benefit from modernisation, but also in those countries which may be adopting or expanding their arbitration laws for the first time. Today, a number of countries on many continents have adopted arbitration legislation based on the UNCITRAL Model Law, although this is more true of countries new to the field of international arbitration promulgating arbitration laws for the first time rather than those who already have arbitration legislation which is in need of modernisation.[5]

[5] The Model Law came too late to have any impact on the new Dutch and Swiss legislation. The Model Law was considered, but not adopted, by Finland when the Finnish Parliament decided a new law which took effect on 1 November 1992, and by Tunisia when it adopted a law on arbitration on 26 April 1993.

Another step to reduce some procedural differences in international arbitration has been taken by the International Bar Association (IBA), notably relating to the presentation of evidence. The Supplementary Rules Governing the Presentation and Reception of Evidence in International Commercial Arbitration (referred to as the IBA Rules of Evidence) were adopted by resolution of the Council of the IBA on 28 May 1983.[6] They are intended to be supplementary to existing rules and only deal with the reception of evidence by arbitrators. They are intended for cases where one party and its counsel come from a country whose system of law and procedure has its origins in the common law, and where the other party and its counsel come from a civil law and procedure country.

The IBA Rules of Evidence can be incorporated into other arbitration rules, contractually, by adding a paragraph referring to them in the arbitration clause, or they can be used as guidelines to the arbitrators. The Rules provide, *inter alia*, for the exchange of lists regarding any document that may be produced during the hearings, a right for parties to obtain a copy of any listed document, the delivery of witness statements within a certain period after the introductory submissions, and a right to cross-examine witnesses.

In spite of the Model Law and the IBA Rules of Evidence, important differences exist in the way an international commercial arbitration will be conducted and in the interplay between arbitrators and the courts at various places of arbitration. I venture to suggest that the differences will continue to exist and that it may even be desirable that they do so, notably with regard to those differences which respond to specific needs for a particular case or specific wishes of the parties.

IV. TACTICAL CONSIDERATIONS

There is no one place in which, in all respects, it is a better seat than others. The problem facing the practitioner drafting the arbitration clause is that he does not know what the issues of a possible arbitration will be, whether they will relate to arbitrability, competition law, admissibility of evidence, examination of witnesses, injunctions, attachments, technical experts or anything else.

[6] Available from the IBA London office.

The draftsman knows who the other party to the contract is, whether it is private or public, the language of the contract, and sometimes the applicable law on the substance. But a future arbitration may become multi-party if a sub-supplier or guarantor makes an appearance, there may be several languages to apply, and the applicable law must be determined.

Some basic choices have to be made when fixing the place of arbitration in the contract:

Active, managing arbitrators or not?
Cross-examination of witnesses or not?
Party or arbitrator appointed experts?
Is effective assistance by the courts available at the place of arbitration?
Are courts at the seat interventionist and is there a risk they will delay the proceedings?

V. ARBITRATION STATUTES AND CASE LAW

Taking a comparative look at Europe, one will find that some countries have recently brought their legislation up to date to accommodate international arbitration whereas in other places legislation is old and development takes place through case law.

London has, with the 1996 English Arbitration Act, the most recent legislation of European cities.

The Austrian legislation on arbitration is the Federal Code of Civil Procedure of 1895 which was updated in 1983. It is thus not modelled on the UNCITRAL Model Law. In Austria parties enjoy great freedom to decide on the procedure as do the arbitrators, see article 587.1 of the Federal Code of Civil Procedure. Austrian arbitrators can actively manage the case, reject evidence at their discretion and cope with delaying tactics but have, as in the other European places referred to below, no coercive power over witnesses.

The French legislation dates from 1982 and is thus not based on the UNCITRAL Model Law. The French Code of Civil Procedure, articles 1452–1507 distinguishes between national and international arbitration. The criterion is not the parties' nationality but whether issues of international trade arise in the dispute. The parties have great freedom to shape the procedure, see article 1494, and the procedure in international arbitration can be totally detached from French court practice. However, where the arbitrators are French-influenced they have a tendency to appoint experts to resolve technical issues and even to conduct investigations into the facts, as is the practice in French court procedure. Information on international arbitration in France is easily available. The case law is reported in *Revue de l'Arbitrage*, which appears quarterly, in French. Articles in both French and English appear in *Revue de Droit des Affaires Internationales*, 10 issues per year. ICC-awards are reported in the last issue every year of *Journal du Droit International*.

Switzerland has a modern federal legislation adapted to international arbitration, chapter 12 of the Private International Law Statute 1988, articles 76–194. The Swiss legislation is not based on the UNCITRAL Model Law. The statute applies to arbitrations where one party has its seat outside Switzerland. Parties enjoy great freedom to organise and conduct the arbitration proceedings. The development of Swiss case law is reported in the *Bulletin* of the Swiss Arbitration Association, a trilingual magazine (English, French, German), appearing quarterly.

The Swedish arbitration legislation is old, the arbitration statute dates back to 1929. A new law is in preparation; it will be influenced by the UNCITRAL Model Law although not a copy of it. Development in Sweden has taken place largely through case law. Great freedom is given to the parties to agree on the arbitration procedure. Where arbitrators and/or counsel are Swedish they will be influenced by Swedish court procedure which is closer to the Anglo-Saxon procedure than to the continental European. It is adversarial, cross-examination of witnesses is a standard feature, arbitrators prefer to take an active managing role and not leave it to counsel to shape the proceedings. The development of Swedish case law and doctrinal articles can be found in the *Stockholm Arbitration Institute Yearbook* published alternative years in Swedish and English.

VI. JUDICIAL ASSISTANCE AND JUDICIAL INTERFERENCE

Parties choosing Paris as place of arbitration can count on a necessary minimum of court assistance and expect little court interference with the arbitral process. Once the courts are convinced that an arbitration agreement exists they will not interfere with the arbitral process. The French word *laissez-faire* is an adequate qualification of the situation in Paris.

Judicial assistance will however be available for the appointment of arbitrators upon the request of one of the parties, see NCPC article 1493. Otherwise courts will offer little assistance, they will not compel witnesses or the production of evidence. Provisional remedies may be sought from the *juge des référés* so that effective attachments and injunctions may be obtained in the arbitral process. The courts in Paris are very experienced in international arbitration; cases relating to arbitration are handled by the *Tribunal de Grande Instance* and the Paris Court of Appeal. Case law is rich and Paris courts have set many precedents guiding the development of international arbitration such as the *Pyramids of Egypt* case (where the Egyptian government was party to an arbitration agreement because of the signature by a minister on a document drawn up between other parties), the *Dutco* case (a party's right to appoint an arbitrator in a multi-party arbitration), the *Dow Chemical* case (an arbitration agreement applicable to non-signatory companies belonging to a group of companies, some of which only had signed the arbitration agreement).

In Switzerland, cantonal courts will assist the arbitrators in obtaining evidence applying cantonal law. In both Geneva and Zurich, arbitrators can grant provisional remedies under article 183 of the Swiss Private International Law (PIL), but they need the assistance of the court to enforce them. A party may bring an action to set aside an award made in Switzerland but if neither party has its domicile or its habitual residence or place of business in Switzerland the parties may agree to waive their rights to recourse in Switzerland with respect to any or all of the grounds for setting aside an award (PIL article 192).

Under the present Swedish law, arbitrators have no power to grant interim measures but can seek the court's assistance for the taking of evidence in court and for the granting of interim measures. Courts will lend their assistance for the appointment of arbitrators but otherwise will not interfere with the arbitral process. Requests to set aside an award may be made if the arbitrators have exceeded their powers, permitted a procedural irregularity, or if they were not properly appointed or were guilty of misconduct, provided that the charge is made within 60 days of the award. Where arbitration is international, the parties may agree to contract out of the right of appeal except for certain serious grounds of absolute invalidity, such as where there was no arbitration agreement and where the matter was not arbitrable; such awards are void under all circumstances. Two court decisions are worth mentioning since they have had an international impact: the *Götaverken* case[7] (relating to enforcement of a French arbitration award) and the *Uganda* v. *Solel Boneh*[8] (regarding the parties' possibility of contracting out of recourse to Swedish courts).

Courts in Vienna will assist arbitrating parties and appoint arbitrators, (CCP art. 582.1), compel the appearance of witnesses and the production of documents, (art. 589) and grant interim relief (art. 589). Courts are not interventionist and an Austrian Supreme Court decision from 1994 in the case of *Dipl. Ing. Peter L.* v. *Dr. Andreas R.* made it clear that the courts should not interfere with arbitrators' procedural orders.[9] Appeals are possible relating to matters of due process, public policy, infringements and the like.

VII. ARBITRABILITY OF DISPUTES

Competition law has, in many countries, been considered an area excluded from the jurisdiction of the arbitrators. Where an arbitrator's jurisdiction is not *a priori* excluded, their powers are, however, limited.[10]

An arbitrator may not apply administrative or penal sanctions or powers exclusively reserved to a public authority, such as the granting of an exemption under article 85.3 of the Treaty of Rome.[11]

A claim that a contract is unenforceable due to the non-arbitrability of issues concerning competition laws raises the question whether the arbitrator has jurisdiction to deal with the dispute or whether he should refer the decision on jurisdiction to a court of law as a preliminary issue. In so referring, the arbitrator avoids the efficacy of arbitration, since the allegation of non-arbitrability may have been made *mala fide* in order to delay the proceedings.

The US Supreme Court decided on 2 July 1985, that a Sherman Act anti-trust claim may be subjected to arbitration where the dispute arises

[7] *Yearbook Commercial Arbitration* (vol. VI, 1981) at 221.

[8] ICC case 2321 of 1974, extracts in *Yearbook Commercial Arbitration* (vol. I, 1976) at 133.

[9] 4 ob 1542/94.

[10] Jacques-Michel Grossen, 'Arbitrage et droit de la concurrence', in *Recueil de travaux suisses sur l'arbitrage international* (1984) Schultern Polygraphischer Verlag, Zurich, at 38, 39.

[11] Professor Berthold Goldman, 'The Complementary Roles of Judges and Arbitrators in Ensuring that International Commercial Arbitration is Effective', in *60 years On* (1984) ICC Publishing S.A., Paris, at 271.

in an international context. This landmark case underlines the liberal attitude towards international arbitration adopted by US courts – also with regard to claims for violations of US securities laws, the Racketeer Influence and Corrupt Organisations Act and the Age Discrimination in Employment Act – and the emergence of an international *ordre public*.[12]

In regard to arbitrability, the French Code Civil article 2060 is unambiguous:

> On ne peut compromettre sur les questions d'Etat et de capacité de personnes, sur celles relatives au divorce et à la séparation de corps ou sur les contestations intéressant les collectivités publiques et des établissements publiques et *plus généralement dans toutes les matières qui intéressent l'ordre publique* (emphasis added).

In theory, since the competition legislation, both the French and the legislation of the European Union (which is directly applicable in France as in other Member States), is clearly of a public policy nature, competition and anti-trust matters are not arbitrable in France. However, French jurisprudence has gradually taken a position in favour of arbitrability with some important reservations.[13] Just because a question concerns *ordre public* issues this does not disqualify it from being arbitrable.[14] Although it was possible to observe a liberal trend in recent years,[15] it could not be maintained that full arbitrability of anti-trust matters in international arbitration was granted in France until the Paris Court of Appeal handed down its decision in the *Labinal* case[16] in 1993. The

12 The *Mitsubishi* case 473 U.S. 614, 105 S. Ct. 3346, 87 L. Ed. 2d 444 (1985); Comments on the broadening of arbitrable issues by Gary D. Sesser: 'Choice of Law, Forum Selection and Arbitration Clauses in International Contracts' in (September 1992) *International Business Lawyer* at 397– 400.

13 Cases Decaux, Cour de Cassation, Chambre Commerciale 21 October 1981, (1982) *Revue de l'Arbitrage* at 264; Phocéenne de dépôts, Paris Court of Appeal 20 January 1989, (1989) *Revue de l'Arbitrage* at 280; Almira, (1989) *Revue de l'Arbitrage* at 711.

14 Pierre Mayer, 'Le Contrat Illicite' in (1984) *Revue de l'Arbitrage* at 206, Laurence Idot, (1989) *Revue de l'Arbitrage* at 299.

15 Frank-Bernd Weigand, 'Avoiding EC Competition Law by Resorting to Arbitration?' in (1993) 9 *Arbitration International* 9, p. 249 at 250, with references to Moitry.

16 *Société Labinal* v. *Sociétés Mors et Westland Aerospace*, Paris Court of Appeal 19 March 1993, reported in (1993) *Revue de l'Arbitrage* 645, comments by

Labinal case answers the principal questions with respect to arbitrability over competition law issues under French law. The decision is as important as the *Mitsubishi* case[17] was in the United States, and confirms that arbitrators have jurisdiction even if questions of public policy are involved; the decision can even be considered to go beyond the sphere of competition law and establish that matters relating to public policy at large can be arbitrated. The decision in the *Labinal* case has been hailed as a final clarification of the previous ambiguity in French law; from now on what many commentators have considered has been confirmed: that arbitrators may not only apply rules with a public policy character to a particular dispute but may also draw conclusions from them in terms of the validity or invalidity of the parties' agreement.[18]

Although Swiss law applied, the Paris Court of Appeal did not discuss the possibility that the arbitral tribunal could apply Swiss law to the substance, excluding the competition rules of the Treaty of Rome. It merely held that:

> public policy rules do not exclude arbitrability; and
> arbitrators may not issue injunctions and impose fines available to state judges.

The Paris Court seemed to suppose that the arbitrators would apply Community rules, but did not leave a caveat like the one the US Supreme Court left in *Mitsubishi*. It is true that the Paris Court referred to the risk of an annulment of the arbitrators' decision, but that was done in the context of arbitrability only. International commercial practitioners who have opted for arbitration in their contracts should welcome the decision of the Paris Court, since allegations of the existence of an illegal trust will not as such suffice to remove the arbitral character of the dispute, even where third parties that are not party to the arbitration agreement are involved. A contrary decision could have opened the gate for (unfounded and illusory) objections in order to render the arbitration clause ineffective.

The *Labinal* decision was followed only a few months later, on 14 October 1993, by another decision by the Paris Court of Appeal which both endorsed it and set out in more detail the powers of an arbitrator

cont.

Prof. Charles Jarrosson, (1993) *Journal du Droit International* 957, comments by Professor Laurence Idot.

17 See supra n. 10.

18 Charles Jarrosson, (1993) *Revue de l'Arbitrage* 655.

in applying article 85 of the EC Treaty. In its second decision, *Aplix* v. *Velcro*,[19] the Paris Court of Appeal textually repeated the general statement made by the same court in *Labinal*: that arbitrability is not excluded on the sole ground that rules having a public policy character apply to rights at dispute; in the international context the arbitrator decides his own jurisdiction with respect to the arbitrability of the dispute in light of international public policy; and that he has the power to apply the principles and rules that flow from it and sanction their non-observance, subject to the setting aside by the competent judge.

Article 177 of the Swiss Private International Law expressly provides that disputes involving property are arbitrable.[20] 'Property' is a translation from the official German language version: *jeder vermögensrechtliche Anspruch* and the official French version: *toute cause de nature patrimoniale.*

Although an issue may be arbitrable under Swiss law, the arbitrator may be confronted in *limine litis* with an intricate problem, namely the conflict between *lex contractus* and a competition law of a foreign country that claims to be the proper law to apply. Contrary to the situation in Germany and France, where it is thought that the parties' agreement in this respect is of no importance and that the competition law applicable on the territory where the restraint of competition has its effect should be applicable, this does not seem to be a view shared by all Swiss commentators.[21]

In a leading decision rendered on 28 April 1992, the Supreme Court (*Tribunal Fédéral*) has dealt with the rights and obligations of arbitrators sitting in Switzerland to examine the validity of a contract under the rules of article 85 of the EC Treaty. The contract was subject to Belgian substantive law and thereby EC competition law; the place of arbitration agreed by the parties was Geneva. The Supreme Court held that not only are arbitrators not forbidden to apply EC competition law, but that they should apply it in order to avoid conflicting decisions; they should not make an award without previous examination of its validity under the Treaty of Rome. The case illustrates the scope of arbitrability under article 177 of the PIL – which defines arbitrable matters in general terms,

19 *Société Aplix* c. *Société Velcro*, Cour d'Appel de Paris, 14 October 1993, reported in (1994) *Revue de l'Arbitrage* 164, comments by Charles Jarrosson.
20 'Any dispute involving property may be the subject matter of an arbitration'.
21 See the discussion following the *Mitsubishi* decision, Jacques Werner, 'A Swiss Comment on *Mitsubishi*' in (1986) 3 *Journal of International Arbitration* 4 at 81.

without particular reference to the competition rules of the European Union, which is not applicable law in Switzerland. It also illustrates the conflict with *lex causae*, Belgian law, leading to the introduction of the relationship of Community law. The Swiss Supreme Court found that arbitrability was to be established on the basis of PIL, article 177, which is a substantive rule of private international law that applies to arbitrators sitting in Switzerland. Thus *lex arbitri* governed the arbitrability and not *lex contractus*.[22] This case shows that the application of Community law is not limited to courts or arbitral tribunals sitting in the Member States. The arbitrators who refused to apply Community law are brought back to heel by the highest court in a non-member country, which thereby indirectly becomes the guardian of the Treaty of Rome. EC law is not directly applicable in Switzerland but becomes applicable through the mechanism of the choice of law rules embodied in its PIL.

The lesson to be learned is that a claimant who is party to an agreement to arbitrate possible disputes and who is anxious to see the arbitration move forward, will be better off in the US, France and Switzerland than in many other places if the opposing party makes an objection to the effect that the dispute is not arbitrable. Whereas in other countries the objection may lead to substantial delays in the arbitration until a local or an appeal court has decided on the arbitrability of the dispute, the arbitrators sitting in these countries need not be impressed by arguments that the dispute concerns anti-trust matters, which were not contemplated by the parties when they signed the arbitration agreement, and that is therefore not arbitrable. The careful choice of the seat, and possibly of the applicable law, may make an important difference to a party wishing to avoid litigation in court on an anti-trust objection brought by the other party to the contract. An arbitration clause may not, of course, prevent the competent authorities from starting an anti-trust case in court against a party, but the arbitration clause will effectively prevent both *bona* and *mala fide* objections on anti-trust grounds from the party who signed the agreement.[23]

22 *V Spa* (Italy) v. *G SA* (Belgium), excerpts quoted from *Yearbook Commercial Arbitration XVIII* (1993) at 143; (1993) *Revue de l'Arbitrage* 124, comments by Professor Laurence Idot.

23 Some commentators have taken a more prudent view on the arbitrator's authority when dealing with an anti-trust matter, see Professor Hans Smit, '*Mitsubishi*: It is Not What it Seems to Be' in 4 *Journal of International Arbitration* 3 at 7. A comprehensive bibliography of the *Mitsubishi* case can be found in n. 7 of Professor Smit's article.

VIII. STATE PARTIES AND APPLICABLE LAW

For a private party arbitrating against a foreign government, Zurich or Geneva or any other place in Switzerland may be of particular interest. Article 177.2 of the PIL provides that if a party to the arbitration agreement is a state or an enterprise or an organisation controlled by it, it cannot rely on its own law in order to contest its capacity to be a party to an arbitration or the arbitrability of a dispute covered by the arbitration agreement. Swiss courts should no longer permit states to decline to arbitrate on the basis of their internal, legal prohibitions.[24]

IX. SEVERAL PARTIES AND MULTIPLE CAUSES OF ACTION

The resolution of all major disputes which may arise in connection with a large industrial or construction project in a single comprehensive arbitration proceeding presents a number of advantages. The danger of inconsistent results, always present where related disputes are resolved in separate proceedings, whether before an arbitration tribunal or before a national court, is avoided. All of the relevant evidence is made available to the tribunal before whom each of the various disputes are brought. The cost of resolving all the disputes arising in connection with a single project in a single proceeding can be significantly lower than the cost of engaging in a series of separate or distinct proceedings.

There are, however, disadvantages. A party may not be willing to have its relationship with his contract party revealed to other parties, which would occur if all the disputes were treated together. Information of a confidential character, e.g. inventions, know-how, marketing, cost margins and financial information are sensitive areas in this respect.

In some countries the courts have authority to consolidate several arbitrations into one single arbitration, even though to join two arbitrations without the consent of all parties involved is contrary to the modern trend in international commercial arbitration which holds that primacy

[24] A recent example illustrating this principle can be found in ICC Case No. 6162, *Collection of ICC Arbitral Awards, 1991–1995*, Arnaldez *et al.* (eds) (Kluwer Law International and ICC Publishing S.A. 1995) at 75.

should be given to the wishes of the parties.[25] Parties are well-advised to inform themselves in advance before choosing a place of arbitration, or when discussing a choice with an arbitral institution, of the risk they run or the opportunities that exist – depending on how the party views it – that their case will be joined with that of other parties even though this may not have been contemplated when they entered into the arbitration agreement. The practice regarding consolidation differs widely from one place of arbitration to another.

In the US, courts have taken different views with respect to the question whether consolidation is possible in the absence of a clear agreement between all the parties. In *Clipper Gas*, a New York District Court consolidated two arbitrations between the shipowner and each of two parties who both chartered the ship, where there were common questions of law and fact in the two arbitrations.[26] The three-person arbitration panel that had been appointed to hear the first case was disbanded and replaced by a five-person panel in order to offer the third, joining party the same opportunity to nominate the arbitral panel as the two other parties had been given.

The Netherlands Arbitration Act 1986 provides for consolidation of related arbitrations on the order of the President of the District Court of Amsterdam. The Act permits parties to opt out of any consolidation of their arbitration with another arbitration.

Consolidation has been ordered also by Australian courts. [27] Arbitration is ill-equipped to deal with multi-party disputes, the Achilles heel of international contract relations.

Paris, or any other place in France, may no longer be such a favoured choice as it has been to parties contemplating the arbitration of disputes involving more than two parties. The decision by France's Supreme Court (*Cour de Cassation*), in *Siemens AG and BKMI Industrieanlagen GmbH*

25 V.V. Veeder Q.C., 'Multi-party Disputes: Consolidation under English Law. The Vimeira – A Sad Forensic Fable' in (1986) 2 *Arbitration International* 4 at 310; J. Gillis Wetter, 'A Multi-party Arbitration Scheme for International Joint Ventures' in (1987) 3 *Arbitration International* 1.

26 *P/R Clipper Gas* v. *PPG Industries Inc. and Georgia Gulf Corp.* 92 Civ. 2181, SDNY, decision reprinted and commented in (November 1992) *Mealey's International Arbitration Report* 9. The decision reproduced in Mealey contains a summary of other recent cases from US courts with respect to the issue of consolidation.

27 Aerospatiale ALZ, comments by Duncan Miller in (1993) 9 *Arbitration International* 2 at 178, 189.

v. *DUTCO Consortium Construction Company Ltd* (the *Dutco* case),[28] will have far-reaching effects on the drafters of consortium and joint-venture agreements.

The facts of the case have been reported and commented upon in various legal journals and will not be reproduced here.[29] The principle enunciated by the Supreme Court – all parties' equal right in the appointment of the arbitrator(s) – may lead to more frequent appointments of a sole arbitrator, where the parties to a multi-party arbitration cannot agree on the persons to be appointed as co-arbitrators.

X. RULES OF EVIDENCE

In international arbitration there is a wide flexibility – or uncertainty – relating to the procedure. One aspect of the procedure is whether a case can be proved at all without certain litigation tools. This problem becomes particularly acute in non-contract claims such as those which have been expanded by the United States Supreme Court in the *Mitsubishi* case.[30] Anti-trust cases can rarely, if ever, be proved by the plaintiff from his own knowledge of documents. All questions of the defendant's motives and conduct are necessarily in the possession of the defendant. The definition of the competitive market can usually be determined only by reference to the defendant's materials and, more often, by reference to the materials in the possession of others. While resort to expert testimony solves certain of these difficulties of proof, the fact remains that many plaintiffs may be entirely unable to prove the elements of an anti-trust claim if they do not have access to materials other than those in their own possession. While the arbitral forum may provide such access in some instances, it is not available as of right at each and every place of arbitration.

28 Decision of 7 January 1992, reprinted in (1992) *Revue de l'Arbitrage* 3 at 470.

29 E.g. in French in (1992) *Revue de l'Arbitrage* 3 at 470 *et seq.*, comments by Pierre Bellet, and in (1992) *Journal du Droit International* 3, comments by Charles Jarrosson. In English in (February 1992) *Mealey's International Arbitration Report* 20, comments by Mahir Jalili, in (March 1993) *International Financial Law Review* 33, comments by Christopher Seppala, and in (1993) 9 *Arbitration International* 2 at 197 *et seq.* comments by Jean-Louis Delvolvé. In Swedish in (1991–1992) *Juridisk Tidskrift vid Stockholms Universitet* 4 at 716 *et seq.*, comments by Sigvard Jarvin.

30 See supra n. 10.

Many claims – apart from anti-trust claims – necessarily require access to the other party's documents and cross-examination of its employees and agents. It is advisable that unless the parties specifically agree on this in the arbitration clause or make reference to a set of rules providing for it – such as the IBA Rules of Evidence – some form of access to the opposing party's documentation, as well as mandatory right to cross-examine its witnesses, be managed within the framework of the arbitration.

It is well known that an important difference exists in the approach to discovery between the adversarial system of common law jurisdictions and the inquisitorial system of civil law jurisdictions. In litigation, the parties have little chance of escaping the system that applies to the court where the dispute is tried. In arbitration there is certainly more freedom for the parties to choose, and to agree with the arbitrators as to whether and to what extent cross-examination and discovery should be allowed. The extent to which one or the other system will apply may, however, be decided by the choice of place of arbitration, where the parties cannot agree and the arbitrator is influenced by local procedure when conducting the arbitration. The influence on the arbitrator may be particularly strong where parties' counsel are local and wish to apply the procedure with which they are accustomed.

England – before the Arbitration Act 1996 – was said to apply the same strict rules of evidence on arbitrators sitting in England as those applying to English courts.[31] The rules regarding the admissibility of evidence were part of the law to which arbitrators – including foreign arbitrators ruling on a dispute between non-English parties – were bound. The English law of evidence includes the parole evidence rule, the prohibition of hearsay evidence and inadmissibility of evidence on pre-contract negotiations and post-contract behaviour. This rigid approach to international arbitration – and the domestication of international contracts in general – has been strongly criticised, since it leaves no margin to foreign business parties accustomed, as they may be, to quite different standards of evidence in commercial disputes.[32]

[31] Professor Roy Goode, 'The Adaptation of English law to International Commercial Arbitration', in (1992) 8 *Arbitration International* 1 at 6.

[32] Roy Goode, *ibid.* The approach contrasts with that of many other countries, including the US where 'there are no rigid rules on the admission of evidence in arbitrations and the arbitrators will permit most evidence to be offered and will consider it "for what it is worth" ', see David W. Rivkin and others in 'Peaceful Solutions', special supplement (May 1993) *International Financial Law Review* 46.

The 1996 Arbitration Act leaves to the parties and the arbitrators to decide whether to apply strict rules of evidence (or any other rules) as to the admissibility, relevance or weight of any material (oral, written or other), section 34(2)(f). This new provision, based on the UNCITRAL Model Law, seems to be a complete change from the previous situation, although one commentator has said that it remains to be seen whether section 34(2)(f) amounts to a substantial change in the law.[33] Section 33, providing that the arbitrators must give each party a reasonable opportunity to put their case, may have a mandatory over-riding weight. The English approach to evidence may be favoured by some parties and disliked by others; it is at least something that foreign parties should be aware of when choosing London as place of arbitration.

The choice of place of arbitration is simultaneously a choice of the courts to which recourse against the award may be available. When selecting France, parties should be aware that a French court, in proceedings to set aside an award may apply its own domestic standards of review of the facts of the case. This happened in the *Pyramids* case,[34] where the French Court of Appeal, consistent with French court practice, gave no credibility to the statement of a director representing one of the parties, even though the arbitrators had accepted that person's testimony.[35] The final result might have been different had the arbitration taken place in England or Sweden, for example, where a reviewing court would not have been likely to disregard findings based on the testimony of an executive of one of the parties.

XI. ADVANCE ON THE COSTS FOR THE ARBITRATION

In most arbitrations, whether they are conducted under institutional rules or *ad hoc*, it is customary to require an advance in respect of the amounts necessary to meet the fees and expenses of the arbitrators and the costs

33 Robert Merkin, *Arbitration Act 1996, An Annotated Guide* (1996) LLP at 59.

34 *Arab Republic of Egypt* v. *Southern Pacific Properties Ltd. et al.*, Court of Appeal of Paris, 12 July 1984, affirmed Cour de Cassation.

35 Christopher R. Seppala, 'The Pyramids of Egypt Case', in (1985) 2 *International Construction Law Review* 180.

of the arbitral institution.[36] It is also customary that the advance be paid by the parties in equal shares.

In practice, however, in a growing number of cases today, the defendant party does not pay its share of the advance.

A claimant who pays the defendant's share may not be willing to wait for the final award and its ruling on costs, but will look for means of obtaining earlier payment by the defendant of its share of the advance. The claimant may then be better off if the arbitration takes place in Switzerland or Germany than elsewhere. Another claimant may not be in a position to pay the defaulting defendant's share of the advance – not entirely implausible in times of recession. He may then wish to opt out of the agreement to arbitrate. In such a situation the claimant may be better off if the arbitration takes place in Sweden.

Claimant requests a decision ordering the defendant to pay its share of the advance.

In Germany, the claimant who pays the share of the advance *in lieu* of the defaulting defendant, and who thus has a claim on an amount due, could request the arbitrator to make a ruling ordering the defendant to pay its share.[37] Such a ruling could be in the form of an interim award, with the well-known effects of an award (enforceability under international conventions, possibility of setting aside, etc.). The claimant's claim should be included in the Terms of Reference, if the arbitration is held under the ICC Rules, in order to avoid doubts as to the arbitrator's jurisdiction to deal with it.

In Switzerland, under the former Zurich Procedural Code article 247, paragraph 3, the arbitrator could order the defaulting party to pay its share.[38] This is said to be possible also under the new Swiss legislation

[36] See e.g. ICC Rules, art. 9; the Rules of Procedure of the Inter-American Commercial Arbitration Commission, art. 41; the Rules of Arbitration, art. 29; the Rules of the Italian Arbitration Association, art. 8; the Rules of the Japan Commercial Arbitration Association, r. 45; the London Court of International Arbitration Rules, art. 15; the UNCITRAL Rules, art. 41; the Rules of the Arbitration Institute of the Stockholm Chamber of Commerce, art. 13.

[37] Peter Schlosser, *Das Recht der internationalen privaten Schiedsgerichtsbarkeit* (2nd edn., 1989) Mohr, Tübingen, para. 778.

[38] Michael Bühler, 'Grundsätze und Praxis des Kostenrechts in ICC-Schiedsverfahren', in (November 1988) *Zeitschrift für Vergleichende Rechtswissenschaft* 87. Band, Seite 455, n. 114.

(art. 183).[39] Other Swiss commentators however, are not so explicit.[40] Unlike the situation in Germany, a provisional measures decision in Switzerland would not be in the form of an award,[41] and thus not enforceable under international conventions. But the arbitrator can, by virtue of article 183 of the New Swiss Statute 'request the assistance of the competent court'.[42]

The claimant is unable to pay the share due by the defendant – can he opt out of the agreement to arbitrate?

A claimant in difficult financial circumstances may simply not be able to pay the defaulting defendant's share of the advance. Because of the existence of an arbitration agreement, he is *a priori* barred from taking his claim to a court of law. The situation is blocked, and the arbitrator will not proceed with the arbitration until the full advance has been paid. Can the claimant treat the arbitration agreement as terminated?

Under the Swiss *Konkordat* this was possible.[43] It seems less clear under the 1987 Statute. In German law the claimant could terminate the arbitration agreement by giving notice.[44]

In Sweden the doctrine is divided on the question as to under what conditions the arbitration agreement can be terminated. Some authors assert that ordinary principles governing contracts are applicable.[45] Others assert that no principle exists in Swedish law which would authorise termination of the arbitration agreement in a situation where the defendant refuses to pay its share and thereby violates either an express

39 Bühler, *op.cit., ibid.* Andreas Bucher, Pierre-Yves Tschanz, *International Arbitration in Switzerland* (1988) Helbing & Lichtenhahn AG, Basle at 86, 87.

40 Marc Blessing, *Die internationale Schiedsgerichtsbarkeit in der Schweiz,* Schriftenreihe DIS, I/II Carl Heymans Verlag at 55; Pierre Karrer, 'Anmerkungen zu Artikel 182–185' in (1992) 1 *Bulletin der Schweizerischen Vereinigung für Schiedersgerichtsbarkeit* 43–44.

41 Blessing, *op. cit.,* at 56, Gerhard Walter, 'Einige prozessuale Aspekte der internationalen Schieds-gerichtsbarkeit in der Schweiz', in *Etudes de droit international en l'honneur de Pierre Lalive* (1993) Helbing & Lichtenhan at 710.

42 Bucher-Tschanz, *op. cit.* at 89.

43 Peter Schlosser, *op. cit.* n. 34, para. 438.

44 Peter Schlosser, *ibid.*

45 Professor Lars Heuman, 'Skiljemäns rätt att avskriva mål', in (1990–91) 2 *Juridisk Tidskrift vid Stockholms Universitet* 317.

provision of the arbitration agreement or the rules to which the agreement refers.[46]

The issue was expected to be decided by the Supreme Court of Sweden in *Jon Warmland* v. *Pro Racing AB*,[47] a case administered under the rules of the Arbitration Institute of the Stockholm Chamber of Commerce (which provide for the payment by each party of half of the advance on costs). The Institute dismissed a request for arbitration after the defendant had refused to pay its share of the total advance of SEK75,000 (US$12,000) and the claimant did not pay the missing share. The claimant took the dispute to Swedish court, which, at the defendant's motion, dismissed the action on the grounds that the arbitration agreement was still in force and not breached by the defaulting defendant, since the Stockholm Chamber of Commerce rules do not stipulate an unconditional duty for each party to pay.[48] One judge dissented, considering that the defendant, having failed to pay its share of the advance, is estopped from relying on the arbitration agreement in order to stop the claimant's court action. The Stockholm Arbitration Institute submitted to the Supreme Court that the situation is a *déni de justice* unless the claimant can opt out of the agreement. Unfortunately, the Swedish Supreme Court was not given the opportunity to decide the case, which was withdrawn by the claimant.

XII. LOCAL RESTRICTIONS ON COUNSEL AND ARBITRATORS

The ability of a party's regular counsel to represent it in an arbitration that takes place outside the party's ordinary jurisdiction, is one important advantage of international arbitration which certainly contributes to its popularity. It is the accepted practice in most countries where international arbitrations are held, that foreign lawyers may appear as counsel or arbitrator, even though not a member of the local Bar or trained in the legal system of the place of arbitration.

46 Åke Hassler-Torsten Cars, *Skiljeförfarande* (2nd edn., 1989), Norstedts at 54, n. 5.

47 Svea hovrätt (Svea Court of Appeal), case Ö3300/89, Högsta domstolen (The Supreme Court) Ö406/90.

48 Lars Heuman in (1990) *Current Issues in Swedish Arbitration* Kluwer/Jurisförlaget, at 192.

There are exceptions, however, to this rule. The best known, because it has been widely discussed, is perhaps Singapore, where the High Court, in a 1988 decision (*Buildings Federal Ltd and Joseph Gartner & Co* v. *Turner (East Asia) Pte Ltd.*[49]) held that a New York law firm could not represent its client in an international arbitration in Singapore. Following international reaction to the High Court decision (Singapore was not a viable choice of forum for international arbitrations and would not be chosen by the parties)[50] an amendment to the Legal Profession Act was made in 1992.[51] Since then, foreign lawyers have had the right to represent their clients in Singapore in arbitration in which the law governing the dispute is not Singapore law.

The question arose recently also in the province of Québec, Canada. It has been confirmed by the Québec Bar that foreign counsel may represent its clients in arbitrations in Québec.

Courts in Malaysia, Barbados and the US have confirmed the general practice that foreign lawyers may appear in arbitrations.[52]

Hong Kong arbitration law expressly states that anyone may act as a party's representative in arbitration.[53]

The recent Tunisian law stipulates that nobody may be excluded as arbitrator because of his nationality, unless the parties have agreed otherwise.[54]

Doubts subsist, though in respect of some countries such as Japan, Korea and Saudi Arabia, which uphold requirements of nationality and/or residence for a person to serve as arbitrator.[55] Saudi Arabia also requires arbitrators to be male and of the Islamic faith.[56] These all seriously restrict the choice of arbitrators in an international dispute and are likely to discourage foreigners from fixing the site in these countries.

49 (1988) 2 MLJ 280 (Singapore High Court).

50 Decision commented by David W. Rivkin in (February 1990) *International Financial Law Review* 11 *et seq*.

51 See (August 1991) *Mealey's International Arbitration Report* 7 and Ang, Cheo and Tan report in 'Peaceful Solutions', special supplement (May 1993) *International Financial Law Review* 16.

52 Rivkin, *op cit., ibid.*

53 Peter Caldwell in (July 1991) *Mealey's International Arbitration Report* 23.

54 Code de l'Arbitrage, art. 56.1 The Tunisian law was promulgated on 26 April 1993 (Loi No. 93–42).

55 Rivkin, *op cit., ibid.*, Caldwell *op cit.* at 22.

56 Samir Saleh, 'La perception de l'arbitrage au Machrek et dans les pays du Golfe', in (1992) *Revue de l'Arbitrage* 4 at 549. Hassan Mahassni, 'General

XIII. CONCLUSIONS

In conclusion, there are still differences in the approaches taken in various countries, as to the arbitrability of disputes, the extent to which a court should intervene in the review of arbitral procedures and arbitral awards, what evidence may be produced, the consolidation of separate arbitrations and the qualifications of counsel. Such differences may have a profound effect on the duration, the expense, and the outcome of an arbitration, and lawyers preparing an international contract will be well-advised to consider carefully the advantages and disadvantages of the available choice of seats.

cont.

Principles of Islamic Law Relating to International Commercial Arbitration', in Special supplement to the 3 *ICC International Court of Arbitration Bulletin* 1 at 25.

5

Leading Arbitration Seats in the Far East: A Comparative View

Jonathon Crook

I. GENERAL OBSERVATIONS

The purpose of this chapter is to identify and describe the key characteristics of the principal arbitration seats in the Far East. The chapter concentrates, therefore, on the Hong Kong Special Administrative Region, Mainland China, Singapore and Malaysia, but is not intended to be a comprehensive study of possible venues.

First of all, two general observations can be made in relation to arbitration in the Far East. As a general rule, the prevailing philosophy in Asia is to avoid confrontation and to seek to resolve disputes through conciliation. This has affected the development of arbitration in the Far East. However, largely as a consequence of increased economic interaction with the West, which has a more 'rights-based' philosophy, arbitration has become accepted as a method of dispute resolution. This is indicated by the fact that most Asian countries have ratified the New York Convention on the Recognition and Enforcement of Foreign Arbitral Award 1958. Conciliation nonetheless remains of considerable importance. So much so that in, for example, an arbitration in China under the auspices of the China International Economic and Trade Arbitration Commission (CIETAC) it is common practice for the tribunal to seek to promote a settlement of the dispute by way of conciliation and the CIETAC Arbitration Rules specifically provide for this.[1] It is only if conciliation fails or is rejected that the tribunal will proceed to issue an award.

[1] CIETAC Arbitration Rules 46–51.

Conflicting Legal Cultures in Commercial Arbitration, S. Frommel and B. Rider (eds), Kluwer Law International, London, 1999; ISBN 90-411-1227-8

Similarly, the Hong Kong Arbitration Ordinance contains provisions which permit the parties to give to an arbitrator the power to act as a conciliator.[2] Although either party may withdraw its consent to the arbitrator acting as a conciliator at any time, it cannot thereafter object to the conduct of the proceedings by the arbitrator solely on the ground that he has acted previously as a conciliator.[3]

Secondly, although *ad hoc* arbitration is practised in the Far East, there is a strong preference for institutional arbitration. This has in recent years led to the establishment of a large number of arbitral institutions in the Far East.

II. HONG KONG SAR

Arbitration law in Hong Kong is set out in the Arbitration Ordinance (Cap. 341). The Ordinance was based on the English Arbitration Act of 1950 but, in a significant departure from English law, was amended in 1989 to adopt the provisions of the UNCITRAL Model Law in relation to international arbitrations.

The Ordinance distinguishes between 'domestic' and 'international' arbitrations, although a number of the differences between the two regimes have been removed as a result of the Arbitration (Amendment) Ordinance 1996. This reflects many of the changes introduced in England by the Arbitration Act 1996. As with the Act, the Ordinance incorporates into statute the principal of 'party autonomy' by providing that the parties to a dispute should be free to decide how the dispute should be resolved and that the courts should interfere in the arbitral process only as provided by the Ordinance.[4]

The role of the court is, therefore, primarily one of providing assistance to and support for the arbitral process. Accordingly, the courts will not allow proceedings to be brought in breach of an arbitration agreement, unless it can be established that the arbitration agreement is invalid or inoperative. This principle applies to both international and domestic arbitrations.[5]

[2] Arbitration Ordinance (as amended), s. 2B.
[3] *Ibid.*, s. 2B(4).
[4] *Ibid.*, s. 2GA.
[5] Section 6 of the Arbitration Ordinance extends the application of art. 8 of the UNCITRAL Model Law to domestic arbitrations.

Under the Arbitration Ordinance as amended, the arbitral tribunal has various powers which it may exercise in both domestic and international arbitrations. In particular, the tribunal may make orders:

- requiring a claimant to provide security for costs (although security may not be ordered solely on the grounds that the claimant is resident outside Hong Kong);
- requiring the amount in dispute to be secured;
- directing the discovery of documents;
- directing evidence to be given by affidavit and requiring the attendance of witnesses;
- requiring the inspection, preservation, detention or sale of property;
- granting interim injunctions;[6]

An order or direction made by the tribunal may be enforced as a court order subject to obtaining leave from the court. This, however, save in exceptional circumstances, will be granted readily and promptly.[7]

The court has similar powers to the tribunal but may decline to exercise those powers if a matter is currently the subject of arbitration proceedings and the court considers that it is more appropriate for the matter to be dealt with by the relevant tribunal.[8] Accordingly, where an arbitration has already been commenced or unless there is a need for urgent action, the court is unlikely to exercise its powers and will require the appropriate application to be made to the arbitral tribunal.

In an arbitration conducted under the domestic regime there are limited rights of appeal on questions of law and the parties can apply to have an award remitted[9] or set aside[10] (e.g. for misconduct by the arbitrator). As would be expected, the courts in Hong Kong rarely interfere with the contents of a domestic award.

In relation to an international arbitration in Hong Kong, however, the rights of recourse against an award are the very limited grounds set out in the UNCITRAL Model Law. In essence, it is necessary to establish that one of the parties to the arbitration agreement did not have capacity to enter into the agreement, that the arbitration agreement was not valid

6 Arbitration Ordinance, s. 2GB.
7 Arbitration Ordinance, s. 2GG.
8 *Ibid.*, s. 2GC.
9 *Ibid.*, s. 24.
10 *Ibid.*, s. 25.

under the law governing it or that the dispute fell outside the scope of the agreement. Enforcement may also be refused if the party against whom it is sought was not given proper notice of the proceedings or an adequate opportunity to present its case.[11]

However, the Arbitration Ordinance also recognises that, in certain cases, the parties to an international arbitration may wish to preserve the right of appeal on important questions of law. The Ordinance allows scope for this by providing that the parties may, by agreement, 'opt in' to the domestic regime.[12] Similarly, parties to a domestic arbitration may 'opt in' to the international regime and thus largely exclude the Court's limited powers of review.[13]

In keeping with the liberal arbitration regime in Hong Kong, there are no restrictions on rights of representation. Accordingly, the parties need not be represented by a Hong Kong lawyer or indeed any lawyer at all. Hong Kong does, however, have a large pool of lawyers and arbitrators with expertise not only in Hong Kong and mainland Chinese law, but also English and US law.

Hong Kong has its own arbitration institution, the Hong Kong International Arbitration Centre (HKIAC). The HKIAC was established in 1985 and is an independent and non-profit making organisation with a modern arbitration centre in the Central district of Hong Kong. It has its own domestic arbitration rules and administers international arbitrations under the UNCITRAL Rules (with certain modifications). In 1996, 197 new cases were referred to the HKIAC.

The HKIAC provides advice, assistance and facilities for the conduct of arbitrations in Hong Kong. However, its role has expanded recently following the recent amendments to the Arbitration Ordinance. It has replaced the Court of First Instance (formerly the High Court) as the body with responsibility for appointing arbitrators in instances where the parties are unable to agree on the appointment of an arbitrator and have not agreed a procedure whereby such an impasse can be overcome.[14] In the past an application to appoint an arbitrator had to be made to the Court. This could be an expensive and time-consuming process, especially if the intended respondent was located outside Hong Kong.

Hong Kong has a reputation as a quite expensive venue for the conduct

[11] UNCITRAL Model Law, art. 36.

[12] Arbitration Ordinance, s. 2M.

[13] *Ibid.*, s. 2L.

[14] Arbitration Ordinance, ss. 12, 34C(3).

of arbitrations. The Arbitration Ordinance now provides, however, that, subject to ensuring that the parties have an adequate opportunity to present their case, arbitrators are to adopt procedures appropriate to the particular case and to avoid unnecessary delay and expense.[15] Furthermore, in the absence of an agreement to the contrary, the arbitral tribunal is now authorised under the Ordinance to direct that the recoverable costs of the arbitration should be limited to a specific amount.[16] This is a power that needs to be exercised carefully by the tribunal but it does have the potential for significantly reducing the costs of arbitration generally.

In recent years, there has been a degree of reluctance to specify Hong Kong as a seat for international arbitrations, apparently due to uncertainty as to the effect of the change in sovereignty. In particular, there has been concern that the handover might have an adverse effect on Hong Kong's status under the New York Convention with the result that an award obtained in Hong Kong would not be enforceable in other jurisdictions under the Convention. This concern has largely overlooked the fact that the People's Republic of China has been a signatory to the New York Convention since 1987 and also that the Basic Law (the constitutional document which governs the relationship between Hong Kong and the PRC as a whole) contains provisions which preserve Hong Kong's status under international treaties. In order, however, to remove any remaining doubt, in June 1997 the PRC notified the United Nations that the New York Convention would continue to be applied in Hong Kong.[17] The Convention no longer applies, however, as between Hong Kong and Mainland China. This is an issue which is referred to below.

III. MAINLAND CHINA

China has a relatively recent history of conducting international commercial arbitrations. The Foreign Trade Arbitration Commission was originally established in the 1950s and became the Foreign Economic and Trade Arbitration Commission (FETAC) in 1980. In 1988 FETAC was renamed the China International Economic and Trade Arbitration

[15] *Ibid.*, s. 2GA.
[16] *Ibid.*, s. 2GL.
[17] Notification by China and the United Kingdom of Great Britain and Northern Ireland relating to Hong Kong, published by the United Nations in August 1997 (UN Depository Notification C.N. 273.1997. Treaties - 2).

Commission (CIETAC). CIETAC has exclusive jurisdiction in respect of arbitrations arising out of international or 'foreign related' economic or trade transactions and the China Maritime Arbitration Commission (CMAC) has a similar jurisdiction in relation to maritime disputes. CIETAC is perhaps the busiest arbitration centre in the world. It received 778 references to arbitration during 1996. However, many CIETAC arbitrations arise from arbitration clauses in standard form documents for trade with Chinese state enterprises which are, in effect, non-negotiable.

The principal sources of arbitration law in the PRC are the Arbitration Law of 1995 and the Civil Procedure Law of 1991. The Arbitration Law primarily governs domestic arbitrations but does contain provisions relating to the enforcement of CIETAC and CMAC awards.[18] The Civil Procedure Law contains provisions which require the PRC Courts to give effect to arbitration agreements[19] and for the enforcement of the awards of foreign arbitral bodies.[20]

As noted, CIETAC and CMAC have an effective monopoly over the conduct of arbitrations in the PRC. Until very recently CIETAC would only apply its own rules, although the parties can now choose to adopt the rules of another institution.[21]

Although CIETAC has stated that it has no objection to other arbitral institutions supervising arbitrations in the PRC, international arbitrations in the PRC under the rules of a foreign institution are in practice discouraged by the absence of any legal mechanism for the enforcement of awards other than those made by CIETAC and CMAC arbitrators. Thus, whilst the PRC courts will (at least in theory) give effect to an ICC or LCIA arbitration award made, for instance, in London or Paris, they would not recognise an LCIA award made in the PRC itself.

Similarly, *ad hoc* arbitration is not recognised in the PRC. Arbitration clauses which do not name a specific institution to administer the arbitration have been rejected as defective by the PRC Courts. The courts have even refused to give effect to an arbitration clause which provided for arbitration pursuant to the rules of the ICC in Paris on the grounds that the clause failed to state that the arbitration would be administered by the ICC.

Accordingly, save where the rules themselves permit it, the parties cannot agree alterations to the rules. This can considerably limit

[18] Arbitration Law, chapter 7, arts. 65–73.

[19] Civil Procedure Law, art. 257.

[20] *Ibid.*, art. 269.

[21] CIETAC Arbitration Rules, art. 7. (2nd revision, May 1998)

the flexibility of the parties to adopt procedures suited to their specific dispute. For example, the timetable set down in a CIETAC arbitration is quite short, which may be appropriate for the majority of general trade disputes but is unlikely to be acceptable in a large scale project dispute.

The rules also provide that all arbitrators must be chosen from the CIETAC Panel of Arbitrators.[22] Prior to 1989, the panel was exclusively Chinese. However, foreign members have since been appointed. As at November 1997 there were 281 mainland Chinese, 24 Hong Kong Chinese and 123 foreign nationals (from 26 countries) on the CIETAC panel.

The parties to a CIETAC arbitration may agree on there being just one arbitrator.[23] There are, however, invariably three arbitrators with each party appointing one arbitrator and the third and presiding arbitrator usually appointed by CIETAC. CIETAC's policy in the past has been to appoint only nationals of mainland China as presiding arbitrators. It is, however, aware that this has been criticised and the practice may change. However, for the time being, in a CIETAC arbitration it is likely that at least two of the arbitrators will be mainland Chinese. It is for this reason that the neutrality of arbitral tribunals appointed by CIETAC has sometimes been questioned.

Indeed, on occasion, the appointments made by CIETAC have been unfortunate. For example, in a recent case,[24] the Hong Kong Court was faced with an application to enforce a CIETAC award in a case where a substitute arbitrator appointed by CIETAC was a director of the Import and Export Commodities Inspection Bureau. The Bureau had produced an inspection certificate upon which the claimant had based its claim and which was challenged by the respondent. The Hong Kong Courts allowed enforcement of the award on the basis that it had not been demonstrated that the arbitrator in question had a sufficient personal interest in the case to call his impartiality into question. It is, however, difficult to imagine a similar occurrence in relation to an arbitration supervised by the LCIA or ICC, where great care is taken to ensure the impartiality of the tribunal as a whole.

In a CIETAC arbitration, considerable emphasis is placed on written submissions. The application for arbitration and the response are both intended to be the main vehicles for the statement of each party's case. The purpose of the arbitration hearing itself is therefore primarily

22 *Ibid.*, art. 24.

23 *Ibid.*, art. 25.

24 *Logy Enterprises Limited* v. *Haikou City Bonded Area* [1997] 2 HKC 481.

intended to permit clarification of factual matters contained in written submissions and to allow the parties to argue how these facts support their case. This emphasis on written submissions means that the hearings often can be very short and it is unusual for a CIETAC arbitration hearing to last more than a few days. Many are concluded within a few hours. In addition, in a CIETAC arbitration there is no process of discovery of documents nor is there any effective method of securing the attendance of reluctant witnesses.

The approach of the arbitral tribunal is inquisitorial and at the arbitration hearing the tribunal itself will take the lead in questioning the parties and their witnesses. The CIETAC rules also permit the arbitral tribunal to undertake their own investigations, to collect evidence[25] and to appoint independent experts to conduct inspections.[26] This power is regularly exercised and the arbitral tribunal will often appoint experts to report on the matters in dispute. Prior to 1994, the parties were not required to be provided with a copy of such an expert's report or given the opportunity to comment on its contents. However, the rules were subsequently changed,[27] largely as a consequence of considerable criticism of this and also the refusal of the Hong Kong Courts in one case to enforce an award based on an expert report on which the respondent had been given no opportunity to comment.[28]

The parties to a CIETAC arbitration may agree to the arbitration being conducted in a language other than Chinese.[29] Whether such agreement can be reached, however, will depend on the strength of the respective bargaining positions of the parties. It will usually be very difficult to persuade a Chinese party that the arbitration should be conducted in a language other than Chinese. The language of the arbitration will, of course, be a factor when choosing the arbitral tribunal.

The CIETAC rules provide that in reaching its award, the tribunal must consider the facts, the law and the terms of the contract, international practices and principles of "reasonableness and fairness".[30] This may not be unreasonable if the substantive law of the dispute is PRC law, which remains relatively undeveloped. However, it is very difficult to justify such

[25] CIETAC Arbitration Rules, art. 38.
[26] *Ibid.*, art. 39.
[27] *Ibid.*, art. 40.
[28] *Paklito Investment Limited* v. *Klockner East Asia Limited* [1993] 2 HKLR 39.
[29] CIETAC Arbitration Rules, art. 75.
[30] *Ibid.*, art. 53.

an approach if the arbitrators are being asked to apply Hong Kong or English law.

There are no restrictions on who may represent the parties in the arbitration. Non-lawyers and foreign nationals are, therefore, permitted. Again, however, the requirement that the arbitration be conducted in Chinese (in the absence of any contrary agreement) does impose a significant restriction in practice on the choice of representatives.

The unsuccessful party in a CIETAC arbitration will usually be ordered to pay all or most of the fees and expenses of the arbitral tribunal and of CIETAC. As a general rule, the fees and expenses are modest. In fact, foreign arbitrators on the CIETAC panel have complained that the level of fees is too low and that this operates as a disincentive to many who might otherwise agree to accept appointments. There is also provision in the CIETAC rules for the tribunal to award the successful party its costs. However, those costs may not exceed 10 per cent of the amount awarded to the successful party[31] and it is common for the tribunal not to allow costs at all. This can also act as a disincentive to instructing foreign lawyers, especially where the amount in dispute is not substantial.

The CIETAC rules provide for any challenge to the jurisdiction of CIETAC to be referred to the People's Court.[32] However, there is otherwise limited scope for judicial interference in a CIETAC arbitration. There is provision in the CIETAC rules for applications to be made to the courts for interim relief in the arbitration and, in particular, for the preservation of property in dispute.[33] However, the application for any such measures must be made to CIETAC, who will then submit the application for a decision to the Intermediate People's Court which has jurisdiction in respect of the place where the party against whom the interim measures are sought is located. This can be a very time-consuming process. In addition, a party applying for such measures would often be unlikely to succeed, given the protectionist attitudes frequently exhibited by local courts to local state enterprises. In practice, therefore, such applications are rarely made.

As stated above, most CIETAC arbitrations arise out of arbitration clauses in standard form contractual documents, which are issued by state enterprises and cannot be negotiated. In cases where contracts with a Chinese enterprise or body are negotiated, whether or not it will be

31 *Ibid.*, art. 59.
32 *Ibid.*, art. 4.
33 *Ibid.*, art. 23.

possible to provide for arbitration outside the PRC will depend purely on the negotiating strengths of the parties. In most instances, the Chinese party will refuse to accept arbitration outside the PRC.

Indeed, if an award against the Chinese party would have to be enforced in the PRC, then it is questionable whether or not it would be in the interests of the non-Chinese party to insist on the seat of arbitration being elsewhere. Although China is a signatory to the New York Convention, attempts to enforce foreign awards in China have to date been unsuccessful, largely because of judicial hostility to non-Chinese parties and a lack of understanding of the importance of adherence to the New York Convention.

An illustrative and well-published case is that of *Revpower* v. *Shanghai Far East Aero Technology Import and Export Corporation* (SFAIC), in which the Shanghai Court initially refused even to accept Revpower's application for enforcement of an ICC award obtained in Stockholm. Sufficient pressure was brought to bear in diplomatic circles to force the Shanghai Court eventually to grant the application for enforcement, but by this time SFAIC was insolvent.

To its credit, the Supreme Court in Beijing is now monitoring the enforcement of foreign awards by local courts, which must now refer to it before they may refuse recognition of an award. It remains to be seen whether the position will change. It is, however, possible that a local Chinese court would have fewer objections to enforcing a CIETAC award against a Chinese enterprise. For that reason, a better tactic for foreign companies negotiating an arbitration clause may be not to insist on a neutral seat for the arbitration but to agree to CIETAC arbitration on the basis that the presiding arbitrator should be from a neutral country. Provided that the presiding arbitrator is a member of the CIETAC Panel, it would appear difficult to object to such a provision.

Equally, it is possible that, following the change of sovereignty, Hong Kong will develop as an acceptable venue for both foreign and Mainland Chinese entities. One obstacle to this is that at present there are no provisions in the legal framework in China which apply to the enforcement of Hong Kong awards. As noted above, the New York Convention no longer applies between Hong Kong and Mainland China. Discussions are, however, currently taking place in an attempt to resolve this issue and it is accepted both by Beijing and the Government of the Hong Kong SAR that the principles governing the enforcement of awards under the New York Convention should continue to apply. The Chinese authorities will, however, not accept any reference to the Convention in any implementing legislation, so as to avoid the implication that the PRC does not have sovereignty over Hong Kong.

Possible solutions that have been discussed include directly extending the provisions of the Civil Procedure Law relating to the enforcement of 'foreign-related' arbitration awards (i.e CIETAC and CMAC awards) to awards obtained in Hong Kong. An alternative proposal (and the approach most likely to be taken) is that the Central Government and the Government of the Hong Kong SAR should enter into a judicial assistance agreement pursuant to article 95 of the Basic Law. This would set out the principles to be applied by their respective courts in enforcing awards obtained in the two separate legal jurisdictions. The intention would be that these principles should mirror those set out in the New York Convention.

Whichever approach is adopted, it is anticipated that the issue will be resolved in the near future.

IV. SINGAPORE

Singapore has become a popular location for international arbitrations, in particular for maritime disputes, and is probably Hong Kong's principal competitor as an arbitration venue in the Far East.

This is, however, a comparatively recent development. Until the early 1990s, Singapore was not a popular venue for the conduct of international arbitrations. This was due to the prohibitions on foreign lawyers conducting proceedings in Singapore.[34] Those restrictions were largely lifted in 1992. The current position is that where the issues in dispute involve Singaporean law, a Singaporean lawyer must be included in the arbitration team. In practice this requirement is rarely unduly burdensome. There are, however, in any event proposals to remove this restriction, which may further increase the popularity of Singapore as an arbitration venue. There are no restrictions on who may act as an arbitrator in an arbitration being conducted in Singapore.

[34] See *Turner (East Asia) Pte. Ltd.* v. *Builder's Federal (HK) Ltd. & Anor* [1988] SLR 1037.

In addition, there have in recent years been amendments to the arbitration framework which have been beneficial to Singapore's development as a venue for the resolution of international disputes.

In 1991 the Singapore International Arbitration Centre (SIAC) was established as a non-profit making organisation to provide facilities for international and domestic commercial arbitration and conciliation. In 1994 Singapore enacted the International Arbitration Act, which adopts the UNCITRAL Model Law in respect of international commercial arbitrations. Domestic arbitrations are still governed by the Arbitration Act, based on the English Arbitration Act 1950.

The International Arbitration Act 1994 includes provisions similar to those in the Hong Kong Arbitration Ordinance, which allow the parties to an international arbitration to opt into the domestic regime if they wish to increase the level of judicial supervision of the arbitral process – and, in particular, preserve the (limited) right of appeal on questions of law – or to increase the discretion of the Court as to whether or not to stay an action brought in breach of an arbitration clause.[35]

As in Hong Kong, the parties to an arbitration in Singapore are generally given a free hand in the conduct of the arbitration. They are therefore generally free to choose the rules of procedure, the place of arbitration, the language of the arbitration and the number of arbitrators.

The arbitral tribunal has similar powers to those granted to arbitrators in Hong Kong to award security for costs, secure the amount in dispute, compel the production of documents and the attendance of witnesses by way of subpoena and to grant injunctions. Such orders are enforceable as orders of the Court, subject to leave being obtained.[36] Furthermore, in the absence of any agreement to the contrary, the arbitrators are given the power to adopt an inquisitorial approach to the conduct of the arbitration.[37]

In 1996 51 cases were referred to SIAC, of which 26 were domestic and 25 international arbitrations.

35 International Arbitration Act 1994, ss. 5, 15.
36 *Ibid.*, s. 12(1).
37 *Ibid.*, s. 12(3).

V. MALAYSIA

As with Hong Kong and Singapore, the law relating to arbitration in Malaysia is based on English law, and the principal legislative provisions are set out in the Arbitration Act of 1952. However, unlike Hong Kong and Singapore the legislation has remained largely unamended since that time.

The one amendment of significance was the introduction in 1979 of section 34 of the Act. This provides that arbitrations conducted pursuant to the UNCITRAL Rules, the Rules of the International Convention for the Settlement of Investment Disputes (ICSID) or the Rules of the Kuala Lumpur Regional Centre of Arbitration (which incorporates the UNCITRAL Rules) are excluded from its provisions. Accordingly, although Malaysia is a pro-arbitration jurisdiction, there is no specific statutory regime for the conduct of international arbitrations. Arbitrations which are conducted in Malaysia other than pursuant to the ICSID or UNCITRAL Rules are subject to the provisions of the Arbitration Act. Thus, for example, if parties to a contract agree that any dispute should be arbitrated in Malaysia under the rules of, say, the LCIA or ICC then the provisions of the Arbitration Act will apply. This has the particular consequence that the supervisory powers of the Malaysian courts set out in the Act will apply.

The Arbitration Act contains provisions enabling the parties to ask an arbitrator during the course of an arbitration to refer any point of law arising to the High Court for determination.[38] If the arbitrator refuses, an application may be made to the High Court who may require the arbitrator to 'state a case' to be answered by the High Court. Before an arbitrator may be required to state a case the Court must be satisfied that the point of law being raised is 'real and substantial', is capable of being accurately stated as a point of law and is of such importance that its resolution is necessary for the proper determination of the arbitration.[39]

Most applications to state a case are unsuccessful. However, the very existence of the procedure can be abused by a recalcitrant respondent in order to delay matters and it is noteworthy that the procedure was repealed in England in 1979.

In addition, applications can be made to have an award remitted back

[38] Arbitration Act 1952, s. 22.
[39] *Yee Hoong Loong Corp* v. *Kwok Fook Seng* [1992] 1 CLJ 90.

to the arbitrator on a point of law.[40] An award will only be remitted if it is clearly wrong in law or if the arbitrator has admitted that he has made a mistake or he has been guilty of misconduct. An award has also been remitted, however, where fresh evidence has been acquired after the award has been made.[41]

An award can also be set aside for 'misconduct' by an arbitrator[42] and the Court can refuse to give effect to an arbitration clause where issues of fraud are raised.[43]

The existence of these provisions and their potential applicability to an international arbitration can mean that the purpose of an arbitration agreement in ensuring the prompt and efficient resolution of a dispute with minimal court involvement could be frustrated. However, the Malaysian courts are generally reluctant to interfere with any arbitration award and as a result, Malaysia enjoys a considerable degree of popularity as an arbitration venue in the Far East. It is also recognised that the legislative framework is out of step with modern developments and the Arbitration Act may well be amended in due course to bring it up to date with the changes that have taken place in Hong Kong and Singapore.

The problems caused by the application of the Arbitration Act may be avoided by ensuring that any arbitration is conducted at the Regional Centre for Arbitration in Kuala Lumpur and/or pursuant to the UNCITRAL Rules, so as to benefit from section 34, which excludes the application of the Act.

A potential problem that arises, however, from the exclusion of the provisions of the Act concerns the issue of interim relief. The Arbitration Act contains provisions which allow the Court to grant orders for security for costs, to secure the amount in dispute and to grant interim injunctions and similar measures of assistance.[44] By contrast, the UNCITRAL Rules are more limited and only refer to the power of the arbitral tribunal to 'take any interim measures it deems necessary in respect of the subject matter of the dispute'.[45] Similarly, there is no clear

40 Arbitration Act 1952, s. 23.
41 *Ong Guan Tech & Ors* v. *Hijjas* (1982) 1 MLT 105.
42 Arbitration Act 1952, s. 24.
43 *Ibid.*, s. 25.
44 *Ibid.*, s. 13.
45 UNCITRAL, Arbitration Rules, art. 26.

mechanism for enforcing orders for interim relief made by the arbitral tribunal.

There are no restrictions on who may act as an arbitrator in Malaysia, although the Regional Centre maintains an international panel of arbitrators. Similarly, there are no restrictions on who may appear as the representatives for the parties.

Malaysia is also a signatory to the New York Convention and will, therefore, enforce foreign arbitral awards in Malaysia, including those made under the UNCITRAL Rules. Awards made in arbitrations in Malaysia conducted pursuant to the ICSID Rules are given effect by the Malaysian courts in the same way as awards to which the New York Convention applies.[46] Accordingly, the same regime applies to the enforcement of awards obtained outside Malaysia as applies for those obtained at the Regional Centre for Arbitration.

According to figures provided by the Regional Centre for Arbitration, during the first nine months of 1997, there had been six domestic and six international arbitrations commenced under the auspices of the Regional Centre which had proceeded beyond the referral stage.

VI. CONCLUSIONS

If the objective when selecting the seat for an arbitration in the Far East is to ensure that the parties have the freedom to choose how best to resolve the dispute and to exclude the involvement of local courts, the principal choice between the seats covered in this chapter is between Hong Kong and Singapore.

Although its development as a modern arbitration venue is hindered by its out-dated legal framework, Malaysia cannot be overlooked. The rules governing the arbitration have, however, to be chosen carefully according to the extent to which it is considered important to exclude the involvement of the Court.

CIETAC will continue to be a major arbitration centre by reason of China's continued economic growth and the fact that companies wishing to do business with Chinese entities will often not have the negotiating power to demand a seat for the arbitration outside China. It is, however, possible that Hong Kong will become an acceptable alternative venue for

[46] Arbitration Act 1952, s. 34.

such arbitrations and for this reason it is important that the position with regard to the enforcement of Hong Kong awards in the PRC is clarified as soon as possible.

In many cases, however, the choice between particular jurisdictions will often depend less on objective factors and more on considerations specific to the case, such as the substantive law of the contract, practical issues as to the location of witnesses and documents, and the personal preferences of the parties.

6

The Practicalities of Cross-Cultural Arbitration

Ambassador Malcolm Wilkey

I. DIFFERENCES BETWEEN PARTIES COMING FROM DIFFERENT LEGAL CULTURES – ROLE OF ARBITRATION

Arbitration smoothes the way in many aspects. Firstly, the parties are not before a national court, where the foreign party almost instinctively would feel at a disadvantage. This is avoided with arbitration. The procedure of the arbitral tribunal is always more informal than that of a national court. In the case of parties coming from different legal cultures, the procedure adopted can be an easy compromise between that to which each party is accustomed. The tribunal itself usually has power to adopt whatever procedure it believes helpful in a particular case, yet the parties are always free to make suggestions, and an empathetic tribunal should do its best to make both litigants feel at home.

Secondly, the applicable law may be that of one of the parties or a national code recognised for its completeness, fairness, and universal application. In any event, it is nowadays usually chosen by the parties in their agreement to arbitrate, whether that be in an original contract or determined later after the dispute arises. The applicable law is probably one with which both parties are commercially familiar. It is also probably a law which is commercially relatively advanced and full of precedents familiar to both parties. In that respect, adopting the law of a less developed country has its handicaps. It is not so much that the law of a less developed country is so different from the law of the most advanced Western countries, nor that it is full of surprises, but it is frequently full of gaps on critical legal points.

Conflicting Legal Cultures in Commercial Arbitration, S. Frommel and B. Rider (eds), Kluwer Law International, London, 1999; ISBN 90-411-1227-8

Counsel chosen by each side is usually familiar with the applicable law. The parties have a much more flexible choice than if they were in a national court, where their choice of trial counsel would be limited to lawyers licensed in that court. As a practical matter, litigants feel the need to retain lawyers licensed by the jurisdiction in which they are litigating. In multinational arbitration each party usually retains legal counsel from its own country and, wisely, legal counsel from the country of the other party or the country of the applicable law – or both.

The arbitrators named by each litigant may be selected from their respective countries, or perhaps a litigant will prefer to choose a prestigious foreigner who understands the culture and language of the nominating country. Assuming that a party sincerely believes in its case, a highly competent person respected for his demonstrated impartiality and objectivity, who is likely to make a logical, dispassionate and persuasive appraisal of the merits of each party's position, is a good bet as a party nominee, not only to decide fairly but also to exercise considerable influence on the presiding neutral and on the member or members named by the other party.

The neutral chairman should be a prestigious foreigner who has some familiarity with the type of transaction involved and perhaps even the legal cultures of both parties. The presiding neutral should be truly neutral, not only devoid of the interest or affiliations that would disqualify him in domestic arbitration, but also selected from a region and culture different from that of the parties involved. Cultural ties run deep; regional politics, both national and professional, lurk beneath the surface of ostensibly even-handed diplomatic amenities. One disillusioning experience will be enough to convince anyone of the wisdom of the above opinion. Certainly the analysis of the qualifications desired in the arbitrators ranks at the very top of the decisions a party must make in initiating an arbitration. Only once this is established should the parties search for the individuals who may fulfil those desired qualifications.

The choice of the administering organisation, if one is desired, is of considerable practical importance. Such organisations vary widely in the scope of services they offer. Some merely facilitate the choice of arbitrators and then retire from the scene. Others have a boutique of suggested procedures and methods of analysis of varied cases which are helpful. Others go farther and control – or are required to be advised of – each step of the proceedings, determine if the award is in a form to meet international and national standards for enforcement, pay the expenses of the arbitration from a common fund, and at the end fix the fees of the arbitrators. It is up to the parties to decide which of any of these type of services they want.

Since it is arbitration with cross-cultural currents that is being discussed, an international organisation to administer the case has some advantages. Theoretically, the international organisation is accustomed to dealing with a variety of cultures, currencies, bureaucratic regimes, all of which should be checked out before commitment. If a national organisation is chosen, it should be one which has had experience with arbitration involving alien legal cultures, which may be vastly different from the local laws and courts. The expectations of parties in a transnational multi-cultural arbitration may vary considerably from a local dispute, and the administering organisation should be cognisant of and prepared to meet them.

As for the Rules for the conduct of the arbitration once it starts, the choice of administering institution makes very little difference, as Professor Lowenfeld points out in his chapter in this volume.[1] The 'Rules governing the Proceeding' of nearly all arbitration organisations are sketchy and leave it up to the arbitrators effectively to make the rules. This works well with experienced arbitrators and counsel. Neophyte arbitrators, however: those with neither much arbitration nor judicial experience, or counsel with a propensity to argue points of order on the basis of much technical procedural experience, could diminish drastically the efficiency and value of an arbitral proceeding. It is not likely that an award would be subject to challenge so long as the tribunal demonstrably applied the well understood Anglo-American principles of due process: due notice, a fair exchange of pleadings and fact contentions, equal and adequate opportunity to be heard, adequate chance for cross-examination and oral argument, no demonstrated bias on the part of any arbitrator.

On the subject of rules, I agree with Professor Lowenfeld that the Anglo-American tradition of oral hearings is now firmly established, along with the recognition that cross-examination is the best way to get at the truth.[2] The question now is whether this will spill over to be applied in civil law legal systems. In the last 12 years, I have seen definite evidence of this in at least two South American countries.

[1] See p. 19 of this book.
[2] See p. 24 of this book.

Once the proceedings get under way, a language difference is probably the first dissimilarity encountered by the parties. Correspondence is no problem, but pleadings, exhibits, documents exchanged, and the language of the hearings are another matter. The parties must agree on one language into which all written matter will be translated, and in which the hearings will be conducted. Neither the language of the site nor that of the applicable law is automatically to be preferred. For example, while a contract may prescribe the law applicable to be that of Argentina, and the site chosen for the arbitration could be Paris, because the contract and associated documents, as well as the anticipated witnesses, are in English or will use English, the whole proceeding may very well be in English. The choice to be made is one of comparative utility, the ultimate objective to conduct a proceeding and form a lucid record on which an intelligent decision can be made with the least difficulty for all persons concerned.

Obviously, where language is a cross-cultural factor, arbitration is more flexible than a national court. A court must conduct proceedings and create a record in the national language. Translation and interpretation under the auspices of the court follows a set formula. In arbitration, both can be more flexible. The arbitral tribunal may understand both parties' languages. If both sides are willing, translation of some documents can be dispensed with on the understanding that either party or tribunal member can call for a translation into the agreed language of the proceedings at any time. Witnesses may feel more comfortable, and interpretation can be arranged in a variety of ways, so long as the ultimate record is put right by the reporter for the tribunal.

II. AND IF THE DIFFERENT LEGAL CULTURES REPRESENTED BY THE PARTIES ARE ALSO DIFFERENT GOVERNMENTS?

The differences between the legal cultures are often magnified when governments themselves or their administrative agency representatives are the litigants. Three experiences will illustrate the varied differences which may arise. One involved a loss of life. Another involved government economic policies in regard to a certain industry. The third involved a government agency making an ordinary commercial purchase.

A. Loss of Life

How is life valued? In the United States and Europe, there are tables on the earning power of men and women in different professions and different ages over a period of years. From such tables it is easy to calculate how much a man of 42 engaged in a large metropolitan law practice might earn over the rest of his life. Other tables give the appropriate discount for present value of such earnings, etc. There are also precedents on the valuation of pain and suffering, the loss of companionship, to a wife or to the children. In other parts of the world there is nothing like this. Human life indeed is valued very low on the scale of damages.

Whose value is to be taken of the life or lives which were lost? The jurisdiction where the lives were lost? Where the deceased. was working? The country of which the deceased was a citizen? What about the position of refugees, who never expect to go back to their home country? What about a stateless person? The how and the where of valuing life illustrate that legal cross-cultures become economic cross-cultures, and must be answered on both legal and economic grounds.

Precedents can be misleading in this field. International arbitration tribunals may be dealing with totally different factors in each individual case. In one case involving loss of life, eventually valued at several million, a case was cited to the tribunal in which an international court awarded $80,000 for the loss of life of a man whose remaining life expectancy was 25 years. This tragedy occurred in a less developed country, where all the participants were citizens and residents of that country, although because international human rights were involved, the case went before an international tribunal. This $80,000 award for loss of life with 25 years life expectancy was not remotely comparable to the values in either country involved in the later litigation.

In the loss of life cases I think there is a bracket of reasonableness which should be used as a criteria. The tribunal should keep in mind that the overall aim of the arbitration is not only to do justice to the injured individuals in the case, but also to remove a potent source of irritation between the two countries. The award ideally should therefore not only do justice to the individual parties, but also be acceptable in both countries as visibly doing justice. Otherwise the source of the international friction will remain and the arbitration will have failed in its ultimate broad purpose.

Where loss of life is involved the general caution not to select as a chairman a person who comes from one of the cultures involved is particularly great. Not only may divergent legal and social cultures play a part, but regional politics may become involved.

B. Government Economic Policies Affecting Certain Industries

This type of arbitration case is now likely to go to the World Trade Organisation. Under the WTO rules, the parties are able to select arbitrators from a panel composed entirely of semi-permanent arbitrators drawn from a neutral country. This is fine, but the litigants should be careful to watch for regional or economic bias. If the arbitrators are drawn from the countries involved, it is very clear that they will be likely to interpret the correctness of economic measures which a particular country takes from the point of view of their own economic bias and cultural experience. The same may be true of arbitrators coming from the same region as one of the parties. The sophisticated litigant should therefore certainly ask for arbitrators from other regions.

The original US–Canada Free Trade Agreement has settled disputes with judges and experts drawn from the two contesting countries. Many people have found that this mechanism has not performed satisfactorily in some cases. Now under NAFTA, with at least three countries involved, the judges and experts will be drawn from the contesting countries plus the neutral third country. As a fourth and then a fifth country is added to NAFTA, this dispute settlement mechanism will become more and more unsatisfactory as it becomes a hydra-headed monster of representatives from each country in the trade treaty.

This whole quirky, freakish mechanism was devised because the member countries distrusted the national courts of each country where powerful economic policies were involved. It is strange that anyone ever expected tribunals composed of private experts or national judges, as on these *ad hoc* tribunals, to be more impartial and trustworthy than national judges serving lifetime appointments. My strong recommendation, made repeatedly elsewhere, is that the members of NAFTA, whatever their number, adopt the World Trade Organisation dispute settlement mechanism for disputes arising under NAFTA.

C. An Ordinary Commercial Purchase in Another Country by a Government Agency

When and if disputes arise, the critical influences may be behind the scenes in the purchasing country. This makes the case harder to deal with from both the litigants' and the arbitrators' point of view. Domestic political considerations and the reputation of individual officials may be at stake. At the same time, the influence of international trade practices as a precedent may be less. Their persuasive power with the parties – and the parties' ultimate masters – cannot be relied upon. Furthermore, while an award may be thoroughly acceptable as being within the bracket of reasonableness in the international commercial community, it is difficult to estimate accurately its acceptability in the purchasing country where politics and personalities may play a major role.

All in all, the arbitral tribunal's task of bridging the cultural gaps is more difficult in this type of case. For example, the choice of law made may have been a matter, not of commercial legal logic, but of national pride, or it may have even been required in government contracts by the law of the purchasing country. The law itself may be shot full of gaps, as underdeveloped as the country. All of which means that an international private arbitrational process should be much more acceptable to the litigating parties than the decree of a national court of either country. In other words, international arbitration is probably the single best device to bridge the differences in the legal cultures of the two litigants.

III. ETHICS AS A DIFFERENCE TO BE OVERCOME

In cross-cultural arbitration, differences in ethical standards are likely to exist. It is not for me to argue here that the absolute highest standard, for example in conflicts of interest, must necessarily prevail. But there are differences, which must be recognised and taken into account by the parties and by the members of the tribunal.

The standard of ethics for the nominees by each party may differ, both in the minds of the nominee arbitrators and in the minds of the parties who selected them. One party may expect its nominee or nominees to push its point of view unquestionably, to argue its position in conference, and probably expect this arbitrator to vote for the party which selected him. In other words, simply to behave as an inside advocate in the tribunal. The other party may expect its nominee to do no more than to be sure that all the evidence supporting its point of view is put on the table, and that in conference all points advocated by the party and all evidence favourable to it will be considered by the tribunal. After that, after all the issues and evidence have been discussed, the arbitrator nominated by a party is free to decide the case completely impartially as if he were a judge on a court of law appointed by the state.

My position has always been the latter, that once all the evidence and issues have been discussed, all of the arbitrators should be perfectly free to decide the case with complete impartiality. This is all that the parties are legitimately and logically entitled to expect.

Contacts *ex parte* after all the arbitrators have been selected and assumed their duties should be forbidden. But sometimes they are not. This gives rise to the suspicion among other members of the tribunal that one or more party nominees may be discussing details of the case, views of the arbitrators, with the party which selected them. This breeds distrust among the panel.

The problem sometimes arises that the two or more arbitrators nominated by the parties will be working from different standards. If so, this is likely to produce irritation, disagreement, and ultimate disillusion by one side to the controversy, including not only counsel for the party but its nominee arbitrator. One possible way to avoid this is for the two parties to get together and frankly recognise that there may be different standards, even in the same legal culture, and agree to instruct the arbitrators as to what they expect in the way of impartiality or legitimate advocacy.

The standard for the neutral chairman is much easier to define and rarely brings disagreement. The chairman has a duty to bring out all relevant facts for each side if counsel and his colleagues do not. The chairman has a duty to be sure that all issues, all arguments, and all relevant facts are considered by the tribunal. He should also discourage the party nominees on the tribunal from being partisan.

The issue may be illustrated by two examples of variations in ethical standards as applied to arbitrators nominated by the parties. In one case, one of the party nominees discovered after some weeks that the other party nominee, a retired senior partner of a prestigious firm in another country, had for 20 years been the principal outside counsel for the litigant who had chosen him. He was perplexed. He had never been employed by the party which named him. He had been employed by one of the competitors of that party and hence had some knowledge of the industry and he presumed that this was one of the reasons he had been selected. He was perplexed because he did not know how the situation would be handled. Obviously, the nominee of the other party, their principal outside counsel for the last 20 years, was not about to vote against the litigant which had named him. He could not himself take such a position, the party naming him certainly did not expect him to, and thus the party who had named him was going into the arbitration with one vote out of three already cast against them, and with their only hope that of gaining the two impartial votes. Perhaps fortunately the case never went to a hearing and the matter was never resolved.

In another case the actions of two of the five panellists, the two who were named by one party, produced an ethical controversy. One of the panellists, during the course of the arbitration, actually accepted employment personally as a consultant to one of the litigants on unrelated matters. The outside matter was concluded before the determination of the arbitration. The second panellist did not personally accept employment by a litigant during the arbitration, but his law firm may have done so. The individual arbitrator claimed no knowledge of the law firm's relationship with the litigant, although he was obliged by the code of ethics under the treaty to search out any possible conflicts of interest. None of this conflict of interest was revealed during the 18 months of the arbitration. Only after the award did investigation by the losing side reveal these conflicting representations by the two arbitrators of the litigants who actually appeared before them. The United States protested that under the code of ethics, part of the treaty, the award should be set aside. The other country claimed that nothing at all improper had occurred.

Now, how does a litigant protect himself against this situation? The code of ethics was of course in general terms, but to my mind was definitely sufficiently specific to define this conduct as improper. The United States had the option of refusing to accept any arbitrators named by the other side without giving a reason. It is clear, on review of the conflicting representation and its timing, that if the United States had been aware of these conflicts, they would have asked for the removal of the arbitrators. One way of doing this may have been to agree upon a code of ethics defining so specifically the duty of disclosure to the other side of possible conflicts of interest, with the sanction of automatic disqualification of an arbitrator and of an award if this takes place, that there can be no argument but that the failure to disclose in itself means the disqualification of the arbitrator.

In adversarial proceedings, cross-examination is the greatest engine ever devised for getting at the truth. So wrote Dean Wigmore. In selecting arbitrators, we have a less powerful engine, disclosure, whose potency can sometimes be enhanced by persistent enquiry. In cross-cultural arbitrations, disclosure, its scope and depth may be a problem because Anglo-American jurisdictions are accustomed to far more transparency, in both public and private life, than are European, Latin American or especially some Asian societies. Two principal aspects of disclosure are important: firstly, a full exposition of qualifications, experience, training, and style of procedure and secondly, where a failure to disclose can be fatal to the validity of the arbitral process, a full revelation of relationships and biases.

How many contested matters has the prospective arbitrator presided over? What is his record of handling his cases in a fair, efficient, and businesslike manner? To what standards of conduct does he subscribe, whether those of a professional organisation or personally? How would he describe the role of the arbitrator, his duty to elicit information, his relationship to the parties? On the part of the prospective arbitrator there must be recognised an absolute unvarying duty to report any relationship with the parties, whether in the past, arising during the procedure, incipient or possible to occur in the future, which might create or imply a bias or give the superficial appearance of partiality.

The extent and thoroughness of this of type disclosure is inconceivable in many jurisdictions. It 'cuts against the grain', is not congruent with the social fabric in many places, where ongoing family and professional relationships are simply not thought of as subjects for disclosure or as creators of bias. Yet such disclosure is an absolute *sine qua non* of trustworthy international arbitration. How do counsel for the parties obtain such disclosure? One way to begin is to ask the prospective arbitrator if he is familiar with the Code of Ethics embraced by any of the large arbitral organisations, or annexed to any of several treaties setting up arbitral procedure. Has he participated in an arbitration in which he was obliged to adhere to those ethical standards? No matter what the replies received, counsel should then follow up with a host of questions designed to elicit information on possible bias, disqualifying relationships, or conflict of interest. Only then can counsel make a well-founded judgement on the suitability of the arbitrator.

Full disclosure is not only a protection to the litigants, but also the arbitrators themselves. A challenge to the arbitral award on the ground of undisclosed bias on the part of a member of the tribunal can not only be fatal to the award but highly damaging to the professional standing of the arbitrator. Courts are becoming more willing to scrutinise relationships among arbitrators and parties and/or counsel in order to ascertain the existence of bias, conflict of interest, or other objectionable conduct requiring the vacating of awards: *Lifecare International, Inc.* v. *CD Medical, Inc.*,[3] *Sunkist Soft Drinks* v. *Sunkist Growers, Inc.*[4] Full disclosure by each member of the tribunal, followed by consent of each of the litigants to each member's appointment, should be sufficient to meet any subsequent challenge to the award.

One really difficult problem is what the post-arbitration standards should be. The conflicts of interest during the actual period of arbitration are discussed above and seem to be a simple matter of judgement. However, what restrictions, if any, should be imposed on the arbitrators in regard to subsequent employment by the litigants? Many jurisdictions have not even considered this. The United States government has some restrictions on subsequent employment in the private sector after a government employee – lawyer or otherwise – leaves the government. These standards have been criticised as being too lax. We have only begun to think about the problem in private arbitration, yet it would not be at all uncommon for arbitrators involved in a case to hope for some kind of employment by one of the litigants after the case is over. This is one of the areas which an astute counsel would wish to cover in questioning prospective arbitrators. Probing – and later proving – the perhaps gossamer dreams of future employment in an arbitrator's mind could be a task of challenging delicacy.

There remains one final problem in relation to ferreting out potential conflicts of interest and challengeable relationships leading to possible bias. The real interested parties may not be those named, the ostensible litigants, at all. In one case, the neutral chairman found that the insurance coverage on both sides was several layers deep in coverage, not only as to amounts but as to time spans during which relevant events occurred and different causation of different types of damage, none of which could be certain until after the proof had been received and evaluated. The claimant had received substantial compensation from its carriers before the arbitration was agreed to. The carriers were in several countries in many time zones, so when something really important had to be agreed to, there were frequently delays. This is not at all unusual, given the manner in which international commerce is now conducted. For the

3 68 F. 3rd 429 (CA 1995).
4 10 F. 3rd 753 (11 CA 1993).

careful counsel and the conscientious, scrupulous arbitrator, these transnational complexities add to their burdens in discovering potential disqualifying relationships.

As should be clear from the above, the reactions of participants in cross-cultural arbitration to the variety of problems discussed will be widely diverse. Realising this, the litigants, their counsel and the tribunal must all be alert to be sure that all participants accurately understand what is being done and why.

IV. COSTS AND DELAYS – PROCEDURE, DOCUMENTS, AND DISCOVERY

One cross-cultural difference which startles litigants from cultures other than the Anglo-American is the costs and delays which are creeping into the private arbitration process. United States society is reputed to be the most litigious in world history, and to rival in some instances the medieval English system in its complex maze of procedural devices. Some international observers believe that the mass entry of Anglo-American practitioners into transnational arbitration has 'banalised'[5] and 'judicialised'[6] the process. 'American style practices have taken off ... [with] more attention to fact, motions, objections [and] delays. [Arbitration is] [b]eginning to look more like litigation.'[7] Obviously, if private arbitration begins to look, act, and feel more and more like that expensive, dilatory, technicality-infested system at the government courthouse which we are desperately trying to avoid, private arbitration will lose most of its alleged advantages.

There are several causes of this. One is that, in contrast to the European system and others built on it, the arbitral procedure has become more elaborately adversarial, following the Anglo-American model. Another is that arbitral rules originally either prohibited or severely discouraged that great invention of the US legal system: discovery. Many arbitral rules, even some in the United States, still do discourage discovery. But federal and state laws on arbitration differ regarding the amount of discovery permitted, ranging from no or limited discovery to discovery as generous

5 Dezalay and Garth, 'Merchants of Law as Moral Entrepreneurs' in (1995) 29 *Law and Society Review* 27.
6 *Ibid.*
7 *Ibid.*

as that permitted by state rules in court litigation. Linked to discovery, of course, is the production of documents. It can be an interminable process: the search, the duplication, the analysis by counsel and experts. The litigating counsel demand everything, keep demanding, to achieve objectives both legitimate and illegitimate.

The author has arbitrated under all three approaches: no discovery, limited discovery and full discovery. The less discovery is allowed, the better for arbitration. This approach would suit non-Anglo-American litigants just fine. It is clear that when full discovery, of the style of the state courts, is permitted, the advantages of arbitration over regular judicial procedure in terms of speed and cost slowly disappear. Theoretically the parties could agree, either in advance or after the issues and dispute occur, to limit discovery irrespective of what the law states. It may be too late once the specific dispute arrives; one side may see an advantage in dragging out the proceeding just as in court. If pre-judgment interest is not likely to be awarded, and if the sum involved is substantial, cold calculation may show the prospective loser that it is cheaper to pay the lawyers to do everything legal to postpone the day of judgment. This attitude of course frustrates the whole arbitration purpose.

Thus the Continental or South American or Asian litigant in a transnational arbitral proceeding may find himself in a world hitherto unknown to him, frustrated by the delays and costs, and eventually pressured into throwing up his hands and settling the arbitration at a minimal figure. And, of course, resolving never to be trapped into such a cumbersome procedure again.

V. THE DISADVANTAGED LITIGANT

Different legal cultures sometimes mean different levels of litigants' resources, a different sophistication in carrying on litigation in court or in arbitration, and frequently an erroneous evaluation of the strength of one's own case. What does the *litigant* do about it?

First of all, the litigant coming from a smaller, less developed country should put aside his pride in his local culture. Pride in one's own country is a great thing and in many cases thoroughly justified, but the litigant's job is to win the case. This involves putting things into the perspective of a different culture from which the arbitrators are likely to come, and also in some ways the different culture of the opponent. The disadvantaged litigant should not blindly insist on applying the local law of his own country unless he has analysed it carefully and finds it to his advantage, assuming, of course, that this is permissible under the arbitration agreement. Other more sophisticated legal cultures may provide the precedents for a more just outcome than an undeveloped legal system with huge gaps in the structure.

The litigant should get counsel from whatever area, counsel who will be most likely to know how to handle all aspects of the case, beginning with an objective evaluation. He must recognise that this arbitration will be a big thing. He must resolve to commit the necessary resources of executive time and money to it. An unsophisticated litigant may not realise how much executive time (and talented executives are frequently scarce in less developed countries) major litigation will absorb.

The litigant should look around for experts on technical matters who will be convincing to the arbitral tribunal. The instinct will be to go to experts that the litigant may know from personal contacts, but this may not be sufficient. The litigant must look at it from the point of view the tribunal is likely to take; he must consider whether the tribunal is going to find the technical expert convincing, based on the expert's background of employment and specialised knowledge. For example, to take an extreme case, it would usually be fatal, on a complicated engineering question, to put up 'an expert' who came from a Central African republic against experts employed by the other side drawn from, for example, recently retired top engineering executives from British Aerospace or Siemens. The disadvantaged litigant must resolve from the start to find both counsel and expert witnesses who will be the equivalent in quality and credibility to those expected from his opponent.

What can the arbitrator do about it? The arbitrator is a judge, not counsel for either litigant. But the arbitral tribunal does have a duty to get all facts out on the table. This may mean more guidance from the tribunal as to what is important in the way of evidence and issues. It may mean pulling out more facts by more questioning from the tribunal. But members of the arbitral tribunal can only go so far in helping to balance fairly the presentation of the available facts for either party. In one case, a United States District Judge was obviously being very sympathetic to a young and inexperienced lawyer who was having some difficulty in making his case. After the lawyers on the other side had listened for a period of time to the presentation in court, one nudged his colleague and whispered: 'If that young lawyer will just let him, Judge Allred will win his case for him.' Members of the tribunal can not go that far. Recognising that all the evidence may not be out on the table, and that some issues have not been properly evaluated, members of the tribunal can make an effort to bring them out, but must stop short of becoming an advocate for either party.

The arbitral tribunal can help both sides by giving guidance through interim opinions, written or oral. Such opinions can tell the parties where they are at that moment with the tribunal, without making any decision on the final decisive issues. They help the parties estimate their own case and the strength of the opposition. Although the prime objective of giving such interim opinions is not designed to produce a settlement, it is conceivable that the practice may have that effect. A settlement with informed parties, informed as to an objective appraisal of key points of their case, can be more just than an award made by the arbitral tribunal itself. Probably this technique of interim opinions is only possible in large cases which are susceptible to division into parts, i.e. successive hearings on different issues, after which the tribunal not only decides certain preliminary issues but also advises the parties in what direction the tribunal thinks the evidence is leading.

VI. IMPACT OF THE MULTINATIONAL CORPORATION

The multinational corporation has proved the greatest invention for cross-cultural standardisation. In methods of doing business, organisation and administration, business machines and language, the multinational has promoted common usage. Business transactions, such as transnational partnerships or joint ventures, between foreign investors and host countries, have been standardised, and expectations from these and other common types of business deals have been clarified. In the legal field, contract terms and their interpretations have become standard, not only as to interpretation, but also in the practice of employing common contract terms, which makes for international trade and investment stability. All of these practices are homogenising business cultures and eliminating problems of divergent legal cultures.

In 1995, 40 per cent of all international trade was really inter-company trade, i.e., between units of the same company. Ford builds some of its engines in Britain and puts them into a car in Detroit. This inevitably means that business practices within the same multinational corporation have been, or are being, standardised. This inevitably affects competitors in the same industry in every country where the multinational operates. If the techniques of the multinational are superior, competitors around the world must themselves adopt them in order to stay competitive.

Thus while some cultural differences will remain, both in business practice and in the legal area, cultural differences in key factors of cross-cultural arbitration will eventually be greatly reduced.

VII. DISPUTE SETTLEMENT PROCEDURE WITH NON-BINDING DECISIONS

So far, we have been dealing with arbitration, a private judicial proceeding, implying a binding decision determining the interest, usually monetary, of the litigating parties. This is normal and acceptable where the dominant culture is accustomed to rather rigid rules of procedure and decision, and is quite comfortable with them and the decision derived from them. When one considers the cultural differences, however, which exist around the globe, one must realise that these cultural differences may call for something less than the procedure and decision which we in the Western world, particularly the Anglo-American part of it, find agreeable and useful. Mediation or conciliation may be more acceptable and effective.

Mediation for some avoids the embarrassment of the losing party being shown so clearly to be wrong, and compelled to pay a penalty for it. In other words, it saves face. One useful type of mediation is the mini-trial, which exposes the strengths and weaknesses of both sides to the ultimate decision-makers of the two parties. The procedure is that the mediator, perhaps assisted by one or two representatives of each party, conducts a mini-trial, during which the respective parties, through their counsel and witnesses, present their case, just as they would in court. The evidence is somewhat abbreviated, rules of exclusion are relaxed or even non-existent, the neutral mediator rules on irrelevancies, etc. Those present include not only counsel, witnesses and consulting experts for both sides, but also top executives, who will be called upon to make the decision in regard to litigation, arbitration, or settlement. The result is usually a surprise to both parties in some respects, such as the real strength of their opponent's case, and some deplorable weaknesses in their own. Both parties now have a realistic basis on which to negotiate a settlement. No judgment is expressed by the mediator unless he is asked to do so, and very rarely is such an expression by the mediator binding in any way. All proceedings are completely confidential and are not available for use in subsequent proceedings, whether in court or in arbitration.

Another type of mediation, differing in style from the mini-trial, is conciliation. Here, the mediator frequently goes back and forth between the parties, ascertaining their points of view and common bases of agreement, and may from time to time call the parties jointly before him to discuss what would be useful.

The usefulness of some type of dispute settlement with a less binding result than those in strict, court type arbitration is apparent when we look at the cultures of the Far East. Gone are the comfortable common cultural grounds, particularly in law, which we take for granted in Europe and the Western hemisphere, divergent as those regions are. This may explain why the United States' most sharply contentious trade disputes recently have been with Japan, China, and Indonesia. Asians prefer vaguer, more 'flexible' arrangements and informal processes. Does this mean that formal arbitration cannot work at all? Not necessarily, but along the lines of mediation would seem more acceptable to Asians. This is particularly true when we consider that the problems are not so much 'disputes' as highly charged negotiations. The issues may really not be suited to standard Western arbitration proceedings. The determining factors may ultimately not be who is right or wrong as a matter of law, but who has the economic and political power to prevail in the dispute/negotiation.

Yet one cannot overlook the very real fact that frequently one is dealing with billion dollar foreign direct investment projects, and something less ethereal than the 'voluntary conciliation service', recommended by APEC at its conference in Bogor, Indonesia, will be required. Even though the APEC states are not ready for WTO or NAFTA style dispute resolution panels, large scale Western investors will wish to 'see it all in writing', especially the part providing a mechanism for interpretation and enforcement of the contract before a Western style arbitration tribunal.

This has always been the United States' position on dispute settlement: binding arbitration of some type, especially in investment and financial services disputes. The United States preference is clearly exemplified in numerous international conventions which it has signed. Chapter 11, section B of NAFTA, which among other things rules out the pernicious Calvo clause, permits a challenge to be brought pursuant to the ICSID Convention, the Additional Facility Rules of the ICSID, or the UNCITRAL Arbitration Rules. In addition to final awards, interim measures of protection are sometimes available, as under NAFTA article 1134. There is no injunctive relief. A final award is limited to monetary damages – plus interest – or restitution under NAFTA article 1135(i). These NAFTA awards may be enforced through the ICSID Convention, the New York Convention, or the Inter-American Convention under NAFTA, article 1136.

These are all typical Western European or United States procedures: precise and definite. These are what the West has been demanding – and receiving – in return for direct investment and trade. Now that Asian nations are creating capital on a much greater scale, direct investment and trade is likely to grow between them, governed as they are by the softer, less defined rules of dispute settlement. If the West sticks to its rules, as it is likely to do where large scale projects are involved, then eventually certain variations in dispute settlement procedure will be seen, but also a consensus as to the type of procedure which is best suited to the area and the enterprise involved.

On the subject of the enterprise involved, there is an observable difference between trade disputes which are limited and may be transitory, and foreign direct investment (FDI), which is permanent and therefore demands firm rules for settlement of disputes, including meaningful awards. As indicated above, some disputes of a trade nature are really subjects for negotiation, in which certain mediation procedures may be relevant, while disputes arising from FDI may demand 'judicial type' procedures, favoured by the United States, which finds the flexible negotiating type unsatisfactory. One strange fact is that foreign direct investment is growing much faster than foreign trade. Yet, foreign trade has WTO rules of dispute settlement while FDI has no multilateral rules. In 1994 goods and services from FDI equalled six trillion dollars; the same value for trade was four trillion. One State Department official concluded '... the permanent nature of investment requires an OECD-type, rule-based approach, backed by strong dispute settlement provisions, rather than the adversarial request-and-offer approach typical of trade negotiations.'[8]

VIII. CONCLUSION

Despite cross-cultural differences, not only is transnational private arbitration here to stay, but its use will increase rapidly. On analysis, it is not 'in

8 David L. Aaron, 'After GATT, US pushes Direct Investment' *Wall Street Journal*, 18 January 1995 at A18.

spite of', but 'because of' cross-cultural differences that transnational private arbitration will grow. And it is precisely because of the *practicalities* of the process, discussed above, which insures this. The reason is that there is no real alternative. Commercial disputes and inter-governmental quarrels must be settled peaceably. If negotiations fail, the options are recourse to the national courts of one party, or some form of arbitration. The judicial systems of most countries are increasingly inadequate for domestic civil litigation. Add to this the complexities of cross-cultural factors, and the result is a mechanism totally incompetent for dispute settlements. Transnational arbitration before neutral tribunals is the only viable alternative.

7

International Arbitration May Not Be as Confidential as You Think – Or Want

Jean Reed Haynes

Imagine the following scenario. A new client, the CEO of Super Duper Techno-Whiz, has just left my office, considerably less happy than when he walked in an hour earlier grinning from ear to ear about the 'absolutely great' international arbitration agreement that he had negotiated and signed all by himself, i.e., without the benefit of counsel schooled in international arbitration. Given that I try to avoid causing new clients dismay on their first visit, what happened during our hour together that wilted the spirits of this aggressive, take charge, do-it-for-himself CEO, who we will simply call 'Super Duper'?

We need to start with the facts that Super Duper related to me. He is in the business of supplying a service to customers that is possible only because of the newest of technological breakthroughs. He works through distributors world-wide. Unfortunately, some of the consumers of Super Duper's service – including those in Great Britain – are saying that they have not received what they bargained for. The fearsome word 'fraud' has even been mentioned. But Super Duper knows that the problem is not with the service he offers. Instead, it is the British distributor who is at fault. Unfortunately, the distributor lacks the 'good sense' to see it Super Duper's way. The bottom line is that Super Duper and the British distributor were having very nasty telephone conversations about who was going to sue whom first, where they were going to sue and why each was going to fight to the death to make sure that the court battle occurred on his domestic soil.

And then the light dawned. Instead of getting bogged down in a potentially costly and time-consuming international jurisdictional fight, why not enter into an arbitration agreement? In addition to avoiding the

Conflicting Legal Cultures in Commercial Arbitration, S. Frommel and B. Rider (eds), Kluwer Law International, London, 1999; ISBN 90-411-1227-8

jurisdictional wrangling, Super Duper knows that arbitration is confidential. Thus, neither Super Duper nor the distributor need worry that any proverbial mud they might sling at each other in the arbitration proceedings would become known to third parties (such as the consumers and their lawyers) who were considering suing either or both of them. Super Duper was sure that, by agreeing to arbitration, even the fact of a dispute between his company and the distributor – which was admittedly something of a business embarrassment in itself – would never see the light of a courtroom day.

The wayward distributor was duly impressed by Super Duper's arbitration idea. Consequently, he let Super Duper win the battle of where the arbitration would be sited. The agreement, all signed, sealed, and delivered, provided that the arbitration would be in the United States, in New York City specifically. As Super Duper said to me, New York City was chosen only because of its fine hotels and restaurants.

I had some questions for Super Duper. First, I asked him what the arbitration agreement said about confidentiality. His answer was, 'Nothing. Why would it? Arbitration is confidential.' Secondly, I asked him whether the arbitration agreement referred to the laws of a particular state. 'No,' he replied. 'The arbitration agreement says that the law of the place of arbitration will apply. That means United States law, right?' Thirdly, I asked him whether the arbitration agreement said anything about when the parties can go to court, as opposed to having the arbitral tribunal decide the issue. He explained, 'We said in the agreement that we were deciding to resolve our dispute by arbitration instead of by going to court. So that means the arbitrators decide everything and no one can go to court, right?' Further discussion made clear that the arbitration agreement Super Duper signed also did not designate an arbitral body, or the rules of any such body.

The rest of the hour was spent talking with Super Duper about the issues raised by the arbitration agreement of which he was so proud. As background, I talked about the role that state law plays in international arbitration agreements. We then discussed Super Duper's concerns about confidentiality and avoiding any contact with a courtroom where the fact of a Super Duper-distributor drama could become public. And that discussion, which follows, is why Super Duper left my office decidedly less happy than when he came in.[1]

1 The Super Duper case is clearly a hypothetical one. I know of no CEO who is quite so willing as Super Duper to blaze a trail through completely unknown territory. The case, however, is not totally far-fetched in that most consumers of international arbitration (and many lawyers who do not practise in the

I. BACKGROUND: THE DUALITY OF UNITED STATES FEDERAL AND STATE LAW

The first (of many) mistakes that Super Duper made was to assume that state law would play no role in interpreting an international arbitration agreement. Those who follow the United States Supreme Court rulings concerning arbitration know that understanding the *lex situs*, when the *situs* is in the United States, is complicated by the federal–state duality of laws. If this was not clear before, it became so in 1989 when the United States Supreme Court in *Volt Information Sciences, Inc.* v. *Board of Trustees of the Leland Stanford Junior University*[2] denied Volt's motion to compel arbitration, brought pursuant to section 4 of the Federal Arbitration Act (FAA)[3] and the parallel provision of the California Arbitration Act.[4] In *Volt*, the United States Supreme Court held that by choosing the law of California to govern their dispute, the parties demonstrated their intent to incorporate a California state law arbitration provision. This permits a court, where 'there is a possibility of conflicting rulings on a common issue of law or fact', to stay arbitration pending resolution of related litigation between a party to the arbitration and third parties not bound by the arbitration agreement.[5]

The role of state law in cases governed by the FAA was again at issue in the much discussed *Mastrobuono* v. *Shearson Lehman Hutton Inc.* decision issued by the Supreme Court in 1995.[6] In *Mastrobuono*, the Supreme

cont.

area) are convinced that international arbitration automatically brings with it a guarantee of confidentiality and of avoiding 'court time'. Such beliefs, at least in the United States, rest on a rocky foundation.

2 489 U.S. 468, 109 S. Ct. 1248, 103 L. Ed. 2d 488 (1989).

3 9 U.S.C. § 4.

4 Cal. Civ. Proc. Code Ann. § 1281.2 (West 1982).

5 *Volt*, 489 U.S., at 471, 109 S. Ct. at 1251 (quoting Cal. Civ. Prac. Code Ann. §1281.2). '[W]here, as here, the parties have agreed to abide by state rules of arbitration, enforcing those rules according to the terms of the agreement is fully consistent with the goals of the FAA, even if the result is that arbitration is stayed where the Act would otherwise permit it to go forward'. *Ibid.* at 478–79, 109 S. Ct. at 1255–56.

6 514 U.S. 52, 115 S. Ct. 1212, 131 L. Ed. 2d 76 (1995). Neither *Volt* nor *Mastrobuono* was an 'international' arbitration. Both cases were, however, governed by the FAA. The FAA contains one set of provisions (chapter 1) that governs domestic arbitrations otherwise subject to federal law. 9 U.S.C. §§ 1–16. It contains a second set of provisions (chapter 2) that implements the Convention on the Recognition and Enforcement of Foreign Arbitral

Court held that the parties, by choosing New York law to govern their dispute, had *not* intended to incorporate the state court-made rule that the power to award punitive damages is limited to judicial tribunals and may not be exercised by arbitrators.[7]

Despite the different outcomes of *Volt* and *Mastrobuono*, the Court's rationale in both cases is that it is interpreting the agreement of the parties.[8] This is consistent with the well-established rule in the United States that '[t]here is no federal policy favouring arbitration under a certain set of procedural rules; the federal policy is simply to ensure the enforceability, according to their terms, of private agreements to arbitrate.'[9] But the obvious reality is that it is far from clear that the parties in *Volt* or *Mastrobuono* even knew at the time they entered into arbitration agreements that these state laws existed, let alone that they might become relevant to an eventual arbitration. As such, it is decidedly unlikely that they formed an 'intent' as to whether the law should or should not apply. Indeed, one could readily speculate that the plaintiff in *Mastrobuono* did not intend New York state law to preclude punitive damages whereas the defendant brokerage firm likely had a different 'intent'.[10]

If parties could anticipate every contingency that might arise in an eventual arbitration, and if they could form a unified 'intent' as to how such contingencies should be handled, state law would not be an issue. In that case, the parties could draft the arbitration agreement to express their

cont.

Awards (the 'New York Convention'), 9 U.S.C. §§ 201–208. Section 208 provides that 'Chapter 1 applies to actions and proceedings brought under this chapter to the extent that that chapter is not in conflict with this chapter or the Convention as ratified by the United States'. 9 U.S.C. § 208. (Chapter 3 of the FAA concerns the Inter-American Convention on International Commercial Arbitration and is not otherwise discussed in this chapter.) Thus, an international arbitration award subject to enforcement under the New York Convention is subject to the provisions of the FAA at issue in *Volt* and *Mastrobuono*.

7 The New York rule at issue in *Mastrobuono* is stated in *Garrity* v. *Lyle Stuart, Inc.*, 40 N.Y.2d 354, 386 N.Y.S.2d 831, 353 N.E.2d 793 (1976).

8 See *Mastrobuono*, 514 U.S. at 57–58, 115 S. Ct. at 1216; *Volt*, 489 U.S. at 479, 109 S. Ct. at 1256.

9 *Volt*, 489 U.S. at 476, 109 S. Ct. at 1254.

10 The *Mastrobuono* Court acknowledged that: 'As a practical matter, it seems unlikely that petitioners were actually aware of New York's bifurcated approach to punitive damages . . . we are unwilling to impute this intent to petitioners.' 514 U.S. at 63, 115 S. Ct. at 1219.

intent, and that intent would be controlling. In reality, however, an international arbitration agreement that states the parties' mutual intent as to every conceivable issue remains an elusive goal. For that reason, parties need to know and consider the potential impact of state law, as well as federal law, on their arbitration agreement.

II. HOW CONFIDENTIAL IS A 'CONFIDENTIAL' ARBITRATION?

Super Duper had a very valid concern about confidentiality. One can readily imagine counsel for each of Super Duper and the British distributor preparing exhibits for trial, or arbitration as the case may be, that represent hundreds of hours of work product and that portray in the most graphic way the purported fault of the other party. To have these compelling exhibits (and the testimony that accompanies them) fall into the hands of consumers who are more than happy to seek redress from Super Duper, the distributor, or both would be a disaster.

Unfortunately, the arbitration agreement that Super Duper signed did not expressly say anything about confidentiality. Had he incorporated arbitral rules addressing confidentiality, those rules would have been evidence of the parties' intent.[11] In Super Duper's case, this is not an issue because his arbitration agreement did not incorporate *any* arbitral rules. But even if the Super Duper agreement had incorporated arbitral rules, those rules would not have addressed fully the confidentiality concern that steered Super Duper and the British distributor to arbitration in the first place.

The Arbitration Rules of the United Nations Commission on International Trade Law (UNCITRAL Rules) provide that the hearings shall be held *in camera*, permitting the arbitrators to exclude non-parties from the hearings in order to maintain the privacy of the proceedings.[12] The American Arbitration Association (AAA) Commercial Rules similarly permit the arbitrator to exclude from the hearings any person who is not

[11] See *Mastrobuono*, 514 U.S. at 60–61, 115 S. Ct. at 1218.

[12] UNCITRAL Rules, art. 25(4). U.N. GAOR, 31st Sess., Supp. No. 17, UN Doc. A/31/17 (1976), reprinted in UN Comm'n on Int'l Trade Law, UNCITRAL Arbitration Rules, UN Sales No. E.93V.6 (1993).

a party or an 'essential person'.[13] But although the ICC Rules of Arbitration (in force as of 1 January 1998) contain confidentiality provisions, these govern only the confidentiality of the Court and the Secretariat.[14] Moreover, the ICC publishes its awards, albeit with the names of the parties omitted.[15]

The AAA International Rules preclude the arbitrator(s) or administrators from divulging '[c]onfidential information disclosed during the proceedings'[16] and provide that all hearings are private unless the parties agree otherwise or applicable law provides to the contrary.[17] In addition, the members of the tribunal and the administrator are required to keep confidential 'all matters relating to the arbitration or the award' unless the parties otherwise agree or disclosure is required by applicable law.[18] Thus, the AAA International Rules require confidentiality of the tribunal and the administrator but, again, do not purport to impose a confidentiality obligation on the parties.

The Rules of the London Court of International Arbitration (LCIA)[19] and the arbitration rules of the Center for Public Resources Institute for Dispute Resolution (CPR Rules)[20] offer greater protection. The LCIA does not publish any award – at least not without the prior written consent of all parties and the Arbitral Tribunal.[21] It treats the deliberations of the Arbitral Tribunal as confidential 'save and to the extent that disclosure of an arbitrator's refusal to participate in the arbitration is required of the other members of the Arbitral Tribunal under arts. 10, 12 and 26'.[22] In addition, the LCIA Rules declare that, by electing the LCIA rules, the

[13] Rule 25, American Arbitration Association, Commercial Arbitration Rules (1997).

[14] Art. 6, Appendix I and art. I, Appendix II, ICC Rules of Arbitration (1998).

[15] See Ian R. MacNeil, *et al.*, IV *Federal Arbitration Law* § 44.32.6, at 44:233 (1994) ('In addition, the ICC publishes awards and their accompanying opinions. Although this is done without identifying parties by name, enough information appears so that it is quite likely that those with knowledge of the industry, trade, and the like might readily guess who was involved.').

[16] Art. 34, American Arbitration Association, International Arbitration Rules (1997) (AAA International Rules).

[17] AAA International Rules, art. 20(4).

[18] AAA International Rules, art. 34.

[19] Rules of the London Court of International Arbitration (1998) (LCIA Rules).

[20] Center for Public Resources, Rules for Non-Administered Arbitration of Internationall Disputes (1991).

[21] LCIA Rules, art. 30.3.

[22] LCIA Rules, art. 30.2.

parties shall keep both the award and the materials disclosed in the course of the arbitration confidential except as necessary to perform a legal duty, to protect or pursue a legal right, or to enforce or challenge enforcement of the arbitral award.[23] The CPR Rules roughly parallel the LCIA Rules.[24]

By electing the LCIA Rules or the CPR Rules, Super Duper and the British distributor would have undertaken a confidentiality obligation that a court would be likely to enforce as between the two of them. The question remains open whether even such a provision would have protected Super Duper or the British distributor from having to disclose, under federal or state discovery rules, arbitral materials to third parties, such as the consumer plaintiffs who are their greatest concern.

In the absence of confidentiality protection afforded by express agreement or by arbitral rules deemed to state the parties' intent, the only potential source of confidentiality protection is the governing law. Super Duper was right, in part, in concluding that the arbitration agreement is governed by 'United States' law because it is subject to the FAA. But the FAA says nothing whatsoever about confidentiality. That brings us to state law because the FAA does not purport to pre-empt state law that is not in conflict with it.[25]

Eleven of the 50 states have adopted international arbitration statutes.[26] Because the FAA is silent on the subject of confidentiality, the FAA should not pre-empt these.[27] The international arbitration laws adopted

23 LCIA Rules, art. 30.1.

24 CPR, r. 17.

25 'The FAA contains no express pre-emptive provision, nor does it reflect a congressional intent to occupy the entire field of arbitration . . . But even where Congress has not completely displaced state regulation in an area, state law may nonetheless be pre-empted to the extent that it actually conflicts with federal law – that is, to the extent that it "stands as an obstacle to the accomplishment and execution of the full purposes and objectives of Congress".' *Volt*, 489 U.S. at 477, 109 S. Ct. at 1255 (citations omitted) (quoting *Hines* v. *Davidowitz*, 312 U.S. 52, 67, 61 S. Ct. 399, 404, 85 L.Ed. 581 (1941)); see also *Melun Indus., Inc.* v. *Strange*, 898 F. Supp. 995, 1000 (S.D.N.Y. 1992) (relying on *Volt* in holding that enforcing the arbitration rules under the state law chosen by the parties is consistent with FAA).

26 To date, not a single case has been decided construing any relevant provision of any of these statutes.

27 A number of articles have addressed the extent to which these state arbitration laws will be found to be pre-empted by the FAA. The prevailing conclusion of the articles is that there are very few state provisions that could be found to be in conflict with the FAA and thus pre-emption is unlikely. See

by Connecticut, Florida, Georgia, Hawaii, and Maryland have no confidentiality provision.[28] California has a provision that requires oral arbitration hearings to be held *in camera*[29] and also has a confidentiality privilege for 'conciliations', but this privilege does not apply to arbitrations.[30] Ohio, Oregon, and Texas, like California, provide that arbitral proceedings are to be *in camera* but have no other confidentiality provision applicable to arbitration.[31]

Only North Carolina has adopted a comprehensive confidentiality provision in its international arbitration statute. Its statute provides that all oral hearings and meetings shall be held *in camera*, that confidential information shall not be divulged by the arbitrators, and that unless otherwise agreed by the parties or required by applicable law, the arbitral tribunal *and the parties* shall keep confidential all matters relating to the arbitration and the award.[32]

States that do not have 'international arbitration statutes' have, with only a few exceptions, adopted the Uniform Arbitration Act (the UAA).[33]

cont.

Heather A. Purcell, 'State International Arbitration Statutes: Why They Matter' in (1997) 32 *Texas International LJ* 525; Daniel A. Zeft, 'The Applicability of State International Arbitration Statues and the Absence of Significant Pre-emption Concerns' in (1997) 22 *N.C.J. International L. & Com. Reg.* 705.

28 UNCITRAL Model Law on International Commercial Arbitration, Conn. Gen. Stat. Ann. §§ 50a-100, 50a-136 (West 1994); Florida International Arbitration Act, Fla. Stat. Ann. §§ 684.01 to 684.35 (West 1996); Ga. Code. Ann. §§ 9-9-1 to 9-9-43 (1982 & Supp. 1996); Hawaii International Arbitration, Mediation, and Conciliation Act, Haw. Rev. Stat. §§ 685D-1 to 685D-9 (1995); Maryland International Commercial Arbitration Act, Md. Code. Ann., [Cts & Jud. Proc.] §§ 3-2B-01 to 3-2B-09 (1995).

29 Cal. Civ. Proc. Code § 1297.245 (1996).

30 The California conciliation provision protects testimony, admissions, or documents prepared in the course of a conciliation from disclosure in subsequent proceedings. Cal. Civ. Proc. Code § 1297.371. See also Colorado International Dispute Resolution Act, Colo. Rev. Stat. Ann. §§ 13-22-307 (West Supp. 1996).

31 Ohio Rev. Code § 2712.46 (1991); Oregon International Commercial Arbitration and Conciliation Act, Or. Rev. Stat. § 36.500 (1995); Tex. Civ. Prac. & Rem. Code § 172.112 (West Supp. 1997).

32 N.C. Gen. Stat. § 1-567.54 (1995). North Carolina also has adopted a conciliation provision similar to that adopted by California. N.C. Gen. Stat. § 1-567.71 (1997).

33 The exceptions are Alabama, Georgia, Mississippi, Vermont, and West Virginia. Am Jur. 2d Deskbook, Item No. 282 at 872 (1989 & Supp. 1997).

But the UAA contains no confidentiality provision whatsoever. The State of Missouri is the single state that has added a meaningful confidentiality provision to its arbitration law, which is otherwise modelled on the UAA.[34] Unlike the confidentiality provision in the North Carolina statute, the Missouri provision has no exception that permits disclosure where 'required by applicable law'.[35]

The Super Duper international arbitration agreement did not choose Missouri law or even North Carolina law, so the greater degree of confidentiality protection afforded by the laws of those two states is not available. But even if the law of either of those states were applicable, it does not necessarily mean that a court in some other jurisdiction (federal or state) would rely on the relevant North Carolina or Missouri provision to prohibit *third parties* from discovering arbitral materials in a subsequent litigation.

The cases addressing efforts to discover arbitral materials in subsequent litigation show that United States courts generally permit such discovery. The one important caveat is that, like the arbitration agreement between Super Duper and the British distributor, none of the arbitration agreements at issue in those cases include express confidentiality provisions. (And none of them are described as invoking the law of Missouri or North Carolina.)

Assuming that the court deciding a discovery dispute in subsequent litigation looked to New York law – either because the discovery dispute was subject to New York law or because the court found New York law applicable to the arbitration agreement[36] – the confidentiality protection

34 Missouri has adopted arbitration provisions that are substantially similar to the UAA. The Missouri statute, however, protects arbitral materials from both discovery and introduction as evidence. Mo. Ann. Stat. § 435.014 (Vernon 1992).

35 Compare N.C. Gen. Stat. § 1-567.54 with Mo. Ann. Stat. § 435.014. This distinction is important because, as discussed below, the North Carolina Court of Appeals has cited section 1-567.1 to support the proposition that '[n]othing in the North Carolina statutes governing arbitration requires strict confidentiality'. *Industrotech Constructors, Inc.* v. *Duke Univ.*, 67 N.C. App. 741, 743, 314 S.E.2d 272, 274 (1984).

36 Had the Super Duper arbitration agreement specified New York law, there would be little room for debate that New York law applies to the agreement in so far as it is not pre-empted by federal law. While the Super Duper agreement does not specify New York law, it does say that the law of the place of the arbitration shall apply and the arbitration is sited in the state of New

that Super Duper and the British distributor sought would be unavailable. As demonstrated by a trilogy of cases, the law in New York is that '[e]vidential material at an arbitration proceeding is not immune from disclosure'.[37]

The North Carolina appellate court cited New York law in affirming an order requiring the production of transcripts from an arbitration between Duke University and a contractor when a different contractor

cont.

York. In *Volt*, the arbitration agreement provided that the governing law would be 'the place where the Project is located,' and because the Project was located in California, the Court applied California law. 489 U.S. at 472, 109 S. Ct. at 1252. Assuming a New York court would interpret the contractual provision in the same way as the California court interpreted the agreement at issue in *Volt*, New York law should apply to the Super Duper agreement. Moreover, even if the Super Duper agreement had been totally silent on the applicable law, the law of the *situs* – New York – would likely govern an arbitration proceeding that was in progress. *St. Paul Fire & Marine Ins. Co.* v. *Employers Reinsurance Corp.*, 919 F. Supp. 133, 136 (S.D.N.Y. 1996).

37 *Kamyr, Inc.* v. *Combustion Engineering, Inc.*, 161 A.D.2d 233, 554 N.Y.S.2d 619 (1st Dept. App. 1990). The earliest of the three New York cases addressing this subject is *Milone* v. *General Motors Corp.*, 84 A.D.2d 921, 446 N.Y.S.2d 650 (4th Dept. App. 1981). In *Milone*, General Motors sought production of the claims file maintained by Milone's insurer. The insurer had defended Milone in a negligence action growing out of the same accident that led to Milone's suit against General Motors. In addition, Milone and the insurer had arbitrated Milone's claim against the insurer for no-fault benefits. In the course of that arbitration, Milone submitted medical reports and gave testimony. The trial court denied production on the ground that the file constituted 'material prepared for litigation', i.e. the arbitration. The appellate court reversed this on the ground that the arbitration was an adversarial proceeding between Milone and the insurer and thus the 'work-product' doctrine was inapplicable. 446 N.Y.S.2d at 651. Nine years later, the court in *Kamyr* ordered discovery concerning the claims that the defendants were making against each other in a then-pending arbitration. The *Kamyr* court supported its holding by citing *Milone*. 554 NY.S.2d at 620. In the third case, *Galleon Syndicate Corp.* v. *Pan Atlantic Group, Inc.*, 223 A.D.2d 510, 637 N.Y.S.2d 104 (1st App. Div. 1996), certain documents had been generated in connection with an arbitration between defendant Pan Atlantic Group (PAG) and Republic Insurance Co. Galleon Syndicate sought to discover these documents from PAG's former accountants. The court stated that the documents addressed 'the same issues of reserve adequacy and alleged mismanagement by PAG as are at issue in this action' and cited *Kamyr* in support of its ruling in favour of a production order. 233 A.D.2d at 511, 637 N.Y.S.2d at 105 (citation omitted).

on the same project litigated with Duke.[38] In reaching its holding, the North Carolina court said, in describing the North Carolina statutory confidentiality provision, that '[n]othing in the North Carolina statutes governing arbitration requires strict confidentiality'.[39] In addition to rejecting that statutory provision as a basis for protecting the arbitral materials, the court also rejected the argument that the policy behind arbitration requires confidentiality.[40]

Three federal cases analyse whether documents relating to a prior arbitration should be produced by a straightforward application of the Federal Rules of Civil Procedure and the law of privilege. The first of these, *United States* v. *Panhandle Eastern Corp.*,[41] is the single case in which the preceding arbitration was international in character.[42] In *Panhandle*, the Delaware federal court ordered discovery, holding that the defendant had failed to carry its burden of showing 'good cause' because it had not shown a particular need for protection.[43] Two other federal cases, from Illinois and California, hold that the arbitral materials are immune from disclosure only to the extent that they are protected by the attorney–client privilege or by the work-product doctrine.[44] In each of these state and federal cases, the fact that the discovery sought was of

38 *Industrotech Constructors, Inc.* v. *Duke Univ.*, 67 N.C. App. 741, 314 S.E.2d 272 (N.C. App. 1984).

39 *Ibid.*

40 *Ibid.* The *Industrotech* court permitted opinions and legal theories to be deleted on the ground that they were work-product.

41 118 F.R.D. 346 (D. Del. 1988).

42 One of the defendants there had participated in arbitration proceedings held in Geneva, Switzerland. The defendant sought a protective order against producing documents relating to the Geneva arbitration proceedings to the plaintiff in the United States.

43 *Panhandle*, 118 F.R.D. at 350.

44 See *International Ins. Co.* v. *Peabody Int'l Corp.*, 1988 WL 58611 (N.D. Ill. 1 June 1988); *Samuels* v. *Mitchell*, 155 F.R.D. 195 (N.D. Cal. 1994). In *Peabody*, after the defendant Peabody settled an arbitration with the South Carolina Public Service Authority, International Insurance denied coverage to Peabody. In the ensuing dispute between Peabody and International, International sought, among other things, documents prepared in connection with the arbitration. The court ordered production to the extent that the documents were neither privileged nor within the scope of the work-product doctrine. 1988 WL 58611, at *4. Similarly, in *Samuels*, a California federal court ordered production, except for certain documents that it found protected by the work-product doctrine. 155 F.R.D. at 200–202.

arbitral materials was not even a consideration weighing in favour of protection.[45]

By this point in our discussion, Super Duper looked perplexed. He said, 'But what could we have done to achieve our goal of confidentiality?' As I told Super Duper, it is not clear that the goal of keeping arbitral materials out of the hands of consumer plaintiffs could be achieved. But they could have advanced their cause more than they did.

Given that neither federal nor state law provides the level of confidentiality that Super Duper and the British distributor sought, they needed clearly to express their intent in the arbitration agreement. To some extent, they could have done that by adopting arbitral rules that grant more, rather than less, confidentiality protection. But where parties have very specific shared goals in mind, by far the safest thing to do is to state that intent *very clearly* in the agreement. Nonetheless, even if Super Duper and the British distributor had drafted the most encompassing confidentiality provision known to mankind, it is less than certain that a court would find that their mutual intent overcame a third party's request for discovery. Thus, even the best that Super Duper and the British distributor could do might not be enough.

Super Duper had the good sense to ask whether the result would differ if the British distributor had not conceded that the arbitration be in New York but, instead, insisted that it be in London. My answer was, 'Not to the extent you would like'. At least since 1990, English law has recognised 'an implied obligation arising out of the nature of arbitration itself'[46] not to disclose arbitral materials. In *Dolling-Baker* v. *Merrett*, the Court of Appeal considered a plaintiff's request for the materials generated during a prior arbitration in which the defendant had participated. Relying upon the essentially private nature of an arbitration, coupled with the

45 Commentators have proposed affording at least some confidentiality protection to arbitral materials. One proposal would permit disclosure of the award and reasoning underlying it, but not of other arbitral materials. See Michael Collins QC, 'Privacy and Confidentiality in Arbitration Proceedings' in (1995) 30 *Texas International LJ* 121, 134. Another would apply a balancing test analogous to the balancing test applied to discovery requests for work-product, which permits discovery only upon a showing of 'substantial need' or the inability to obtain the equivalent without undue hardship. See Bertrand C. Sellier and Hal S. Shaftel, 'Confidentiality of Arbitration Proceedings' in (13 March 1997) *NYLJ* at 1.

46 *Dolling-Baker* v. *Merrett*, 1 WLR.1205 (English CA 1990).

obligation implied under English law that a party to litigation must refrain from using disclosed documents for any purpose other than the dispute in which they were obtained, the Court of Appeal denied the request for production.[47]

Three years later, in *Hassneh Insurance Co.* v. *Mew*,[48] the Queen's Bench Division of the Commercial Court ruled that where reasonably necessary to establish a defence or cause of action concerning an arbitrating party's rights against a third party, the award and the reasoning of the tribunal could be disclosed. At the same time, the court ruled *against* the production of arbitral pleadings, witness statements, disclosed documents and transcripts of the arbitral proceedings.[49] In reaching its decision, the *Hassneh Insurance* court stated that because the duty of confidence is an implied term of the agreement to arbitrate, 'that term must have regard to the purposes for which awards may be expected to be used in the ordinary course of commerce and in the ordinary application of English law'.[50]

The third principal English case to discuss confidentiality of arbitral materials was *Insurance Co.* v. *Lloyd's Syndicate*.[51] There, the court refined the rule set forth in *Hassneh Insurance* by holding that disclosure of the arbitral award was proper only where the making of the award was a necessary element in the establishment of the party's legal right against the third party.[52]

The contrast between 'United States law' and English law is clear. Neither the federal nor state laws of the United States recognise the 'implied duty of confidentiality' that is recognised under English law. Thus, had Super Duper and the British distributor chosen London as the *situs* of their arbitration, the law would have implied into their agreement the confidentiality protection that they failed to draft.[53]

47 *Ibid.* at 1213.
48 2 Lloyd's Rep. 243 (1993).
49 *Ibid.* at 250–52.
50 *Ibid.* at 249.
51 1 Lloyd's Rep. 272 (QB 1995).
52 *Ibid.* at 276.
53 Australian law mirrors that of the United States, not that of England. In 1995 the High Court of Australia by its Chief Justice, writing for the majority, stated in *Esso Australia Resources Ltd.* v. *Plowman*, (1995) 128 ALR 391, '[d]espite the view taken in *Dolling-Baker* and subsequently by Colman J. in *Hassneh Insurance*, I do not consider that, in Australia, having regard to the various matters to which I have referred, we are justified in concluding that

Even siting the arbitration in London, however, would not necessarily have given Super Duper and the British distributor all the confidentiality protection they sought. If, after the conclusion of the arbitration, British consumers sued either or both of them in England and sought arbitral materials in discovery, the consumers' request would almost certainly have been denied. By contrast, if those same British consumers sued either or both of Super Duper and the British distributor in the United States, the confidentiality protection afforded by English law would not necessarily be decisive in the ensuing discovery dispute. Indeed, it would seem that including an express confidentiality provision in the arbitration agreement would be stronger evidence of the parties' intent concerning confidentiality than their reliance on a term that is 'implied' under English law.

It thus appears that parties to an international arbitration agreement – wherever the arbitration is sited – cannot guarantee that arbitral materials will not be discoverable in subsequent United States litigation. In the absence of legislation or the creation of federal common law ensuring confidentiality protection, the parties can only do their best. Doing their best requires them to spell out in clear detail in the arbitration agreement the confidentiality protection that they hope to achieve.

III. WILL SUPER DUPER AND THE BRITISH DISTRIBUTOR FIND THEMSELVES IN COURT?

Super Duper said that he and the British distributor did not wish their dispute to become public because the fact of the dispute was something of a business embarrassment. This concern raises a different 'confidentiality' issue, one that would arise even if consumers were not likely to sue either or both of them. When Super Duper asked how likely it was that he and the British distributor could arbitrate their differences without finding themselves in a public courtroom, I felt compelled to point out that arbitration leaves open several possibilities for courtroom time.

The first event that could lead the arbitrating parties to court would be a dispute about the scope of what the arbitrators were empowered to

cont.

confidentiality is an essential attribute of a private arbitration imposing an obligation on each party not to disclose the proceedings or documents and information provided in and for the purposes of the arbitration.' 128 ALR at 411.

decide, or questions of 'arbitrability'. In 1995, the United States Supreme Court issued its decision in *First Options* v. *Kaplan*.[54] It held that questions concerning the scope of arbitrability are to be decided by the courts unless the parties 'clearly agree' to submit the question of arbitrability to arbitration.[55] Thus, if the arbitration agreement includes a clause that says 'the arbitrators shall decide all questions concerning the scope of the arbitration', that contractual agreement will be upheld under *First Options*.

The Super Duper arbitration agreement said only that the parties had decided to resolve their dispute by arbitration instead of by going to court. Whether or not that clause would be deemed to put questions of arbitrability in the hands of the arbitral tribunal is an open question. And because it is an open question, either Super Duper or the British distributor would, under *First Options*, have every entitlement to a court ruling on who should decide questions of arbitrability.[56] Going to court for a ruling on who should decide arbitrability would, of course, make public the fact of the dispute.

Super Duper and the British distributor could also find themselves in court if one of them concluded that it needed to seek a preliminary injunction, or some other provisional measure. Neither the New York Convention nor chapter 1 of the FAA addresses interim relief,[57] but New

54 115 S. Ct. 1920, 131 L. Ed. 2d 985 (1995).

55 *Ibid.* at 1925.

56 Super Duper and the British distributor could have lessened the likelihood they would find themselves in court over questions of arbitrability had they adopted any of several arbitral rules. The AAA International Rules, the CPR Rules, the LCIA Rules, and the UNCITRAL Rules all contain provisions giving the arbitral tribunal the power to rule on questions of its jurisdiction, including the validity and scope of the arbitration agreement. AAA International Rules, art. 15(1) and (2); CPR rules 8.1 and 8.2; LCIA Rules, art. 23.1, UNCITRAL Rules, art. 21(1) and (2). The LCIA Rules go a step further and provide that, subject to enumerated exceptions, by agreeing to arbitration under these rules, the 'parties shall be treated as having agreed not to apply to any state court or other judicial authority for any relief regarding the Arbitral Tribunal's jurisdiction or authority . . .'. LCIA Rules, art. 23.4.

57 Courts faced with requests for interim relief in connection with arbitrations governed by the New York Convention and the FAA analyse whether the existence of a valid arbitration agreement strips them of the power to grant such relief. The results of this inquiry differ, but the vast majority of courts appear willing to grant interim relief. See Charles S. Baldwin, IV, 'Protecting Confidential and Proprietary Commercial Information in International Arbitration' in (1996) 31 *Texas International LJ* 451, 460–62.

York, where Super Duper and the British distributor have agreed to arbitrate, has a statutory provision permitting a court to grant interim relief under specified circumstances in connection with an arbitral controversy.[58] But the question really is not whether a court would or would not grant interim relief; rather, the fact that nothing expressly precludes a party from seeking interim relief from a court opens the public courtroom door.

Finally, there is the realistic possibility that either Super Duper or the British distributor will want to take exception to the arbitral award. If so, the successful party will go to court to seek confirmation of the award pursuant to section 207 of the FAA and the losing party will then be entitled to challenge the award on the various grounds set forth in the New York Convention.[59] Alternatively, the latter will seek to vacate the award. Because the arbitration was sited in New York, the arbitral loser could invoke the 'manifest disregard' standard in seeking to vacate the award.[60] In any of these circumstances, the fact that there was a dispute becomes public as a consequence of going to court.[61]

What could Super Duper and the British distributor have done to avoid these forays into the public courtroom domain? Obviously, during the course of the arbitration, they could protect their privacy by refraining from going to court to challenge arbitrability or to seek interim relief. After the award is issued, the loser could decide not to challenge it . But a party who chooses arbitration over litigation in order to avoid any public disclosure of the controversy cannot rely on the fact that its opponent will continue to value confidentiality above all else if it considers that the outcome towards which the arbitral proceeding seems to be aiming is undesirable. Consequently, the parties need to consider carefully, when they draft their arbitration agreement, what ultimate balance they wish to achieve between confidentiality and the right to resort to a

[58] N.Y. Civ. Prac. L.&R. 7502(c) (McKinney 1996). The granting of provisional relief under the statute is limited to circumstances where 'the award which the applicant may be entitled may be rendered ineffectual without such provisional relief.' *Ibid.*

[59] See 9 U.S.C. § 207 and New York Convention, art. V.

[60] See e.g., *Yusuf Ahmed Alghanim & Sons, W.L.L.* v. *Toys 'R' Us, Inc.* 126 F.3d 15, 20 (2d Cir. 1997).

[61] Even where the law generally accords greater confidentiality protection to arbitration than it does in the United States, a party's decision to dispute the arbitral ruling marks the end of confidentiality. See 887574 *Ontario Inc.* v. *Pizza Pizza Ltd.*, [1994] 35 C.P.C. (3d) 323 (Ont. C.J. (Gen. Div.)).

judicial authority. To the extent that they agree – which they are far more likely to do at the outset than later – they need to craft their arbitration agreement to say precisely what they intend.

To conclude, those like Super Duper, who believe that international arbitration brings with it a guarantee of confidentiality, are wrong, at least if the laws of the United States come into play. Despite the duality of federal and state laws, confidentiality is an issue that receives little to no attention from the legal framework in which the arbitration is set. While arbitration is more confidential than courtroom litigation, the parties to the arbitration have to identify in advance the level of confidentiality they hope to achieve. They then need to state that intent clearly in the arbitration agreement. Only by accepting this responsibility to articulate in advance their goals can parties reap the benefit that international arbitration offers of being able to craft their own rules.

8

Latin American Arbitration Culture and the ICC Arbitration System

Horacio A. Grigera Naón

I.

Culture may be characterised as a complex of typical behaviour and standardised social forms peculiar to a specific social group. One could also describe it as an atmosphere of social beliefs, preferences, expectations and principles common to or shared by a specific social group.

One can speak of an 'arbitration culture' to the extent that those who resort to arbitration, either as parties or as counsel, and those who participate in the conduct of arbitral proceedings and the decision of arbitral disputes (arbitrators and arbitral institutions) share certain ideas and expectations. These relate to such matters as the role played by arbitral adjudication, the type of procedural and substantive justice to be obtained in the course or as a result of arbitral proceedings and the degree of effectiveness or binding force of arbitral determinations or awards. In time, they grow into shared patterns of conduct perceived to be in tune with such ideas and expectations. Such combination of common ideas, expectations and correlative patterns of conduct may well be designated as arbitration culture.

In its present stage of development, international commercial arbitration has become, more than ever before, a multicultural phenomenon. In other words, the cultural approach to the conduct or administration of international commercial arbitrations shared by arbitration users, their counsel, arbitrators and arbitration institutions is not the consequence of notions or ideas exclusively fashioned by any one group, geographically localised in this or that country or group of

Conflicting Legal Cultures in Commercial Arbitration, S. Frommel and B. Rider (eds), Kluwer Law International, London, 1999; ISBN 90-411-1227-8

countries, nor does it trace back its origins to any specific or single legal tradition.

Increasingly, proceedings before or conducted by arbitral tribunals involved in international commercial arbitrations, as well as the type of substantive and procedural justice advanced by them, acquire their own distinct features which often may not be compared to common law or continental law proceedings, let alone the proceedings of any specific country. Consequently, international commercial arbitration culture, shared and fashioned by arbitration users, their counsel, arbitrators and international arbitral institutions, presents itself as an approach to the handling of international commercial cases largely detached from any specific national legal or social environment.

Such detachment of arbitration culture responds to the wishes, needs and aspirations of arbitration users and those involved in the international commercial arbitral adjudication process. The level of uniformity it has attained is proportionate to the homogeneous perception, albeit elaborated within the context of a heterogeneous social group, as to the type of procedural and substantive justice to be attained by international commercial arbitrations and the means to such an end. Indeed, the quality, neutrality and features of arbitral proceedings depend on a number of decisive choices carried out by the parties within the realm reserved to their autonomy or delegated by them to counsel, arbitrators and arbitral institutions as a result of choices made by the parties themselves. It would not, then, be a fair description of the arbitral process today to say that parties resort to international commercial arbitration to evade the application of mandatory provisions or public policy of any specific country. Rather, neutrality and efficiency in the adjudicatory process and the enforceability of arbitral decisions by national courts (fundamentally through international agreements widely ratified throughout the world, like the 1958 New York Convention) are probably the predominant reasons prompting parties to resort to international commercial arbitration.

However, precisely because international commercial arbitration depends on choices made by the parties or, to the extent that the parties permit, by the arbitrators or arbitral institutions, primarily on the basis of the circumstances of the dispute, it is not correct to assume that the multicultural features referred to above will necessarily lead to arbitral proceedings unrelated to the principles and notions of a specific national legal system. Though the approach is multicultural, the actual way of handling the dispute may in the end not necessarily be so. Each case needs evaluation on the basis of its own characteristics and the choices made by the parties. Such evaluation should be performed from a multicultural vantage point, though it may lead eventually (e.g., after considering, from a culturally neutral perspective, *inter alia*, the will of the parties, their nationality, legal background, origin of counsel, language used) to the conduct of arbitral proceedings according to the principles and traditions of a specific legal system. As it has been properly indicated, each international commercial arbitration case should be considered as a micro-cultural environment which is to be approached, for the purpose of organising the conduct of arbitral proceedings, as a *sui generis* situation with its own needs and characteristics.[1] Arbitral proceedings should be tailor-made to properly take into account the cultural peculiarities of the dispute at stake.

Be that as it may, the fact always remains that the very notion of neutrality in international commercial arbitration is permeated with its multicultural underpinnings. Neutrality should be understood not only as premised upon the independence and impartiality of arbitrators but also upon their mental openness and disposition and upon an appropriate procedural framework for conducting international commercial arbitrations. There must be sufficient flexibility and detachment from parochial approaches to permit a number of important elements. Firstly, there must be understanding and consideration of each party's positions on the same footing despite its respective cultural background and national origin. Secondly, the procedure must be fashioned and the final decision reached on the merits, taking into consideration the needs and expectations of the parties, in such a way that a fair decision may be reached in the most expeditious and cost-efficient manner possible. There must be no national bias and the context must be aseptic enough not to permit any party to be specially advantaged in the handling of arbitral proceedings because of its national cultural or legal background. Thirdly, as a result of these features, the work product of arbitrators and arbitral institutions must meet the parties' expectations and persuade them to abide by the determinations of arbitral tribunals and institutions.

To achieve such objectives, the choice of the arbitrators and of the parties' counsel in terms of their multicultural background and approach

1 See J. Paulsson, 'Differing Approaches to International Arbitration Procedures' (Fall 1996) *ADR Currents* 17 at 19.

to dispute resolution is also fundamental and directly or indirectly depends on choices made by the parties. Such choices often lead to arbitral proceedings combining or blending characteristics of both the continental and the common law systems, not only in terms of the procedural rules and principles being observed but also of the type of relief to be granted or the rules or principles governing the resolution of the dispute.

If such requirements are met, the chances are that the award and the arbitral proceedings leading to it will be perceived by the parties as being fair and impartial. Accordingly, such an award is likely to be enforced spontaneously by the parties and therefore free from serious challenge before the national courts.

Therefore, if considered from the perspective of the quality, neutrality and effectiveness of international commercial arbitral proceedings and their outcomes, it is not really very important where they take place, provided that they are reasonably shielded from interference from national courts and have adequate support from local judiciaries.

This latter aspect brings us to another important characteristic of international commercial arbitration culture: its development would not have been possible, and remains largely dependent upon, the benevolent eye, and the active support, of national courts and legal orders. In other words, for such a culture to blossom and expand, it needs to be shared by, or at least seen as deserving support from, national legislative bodies, judiciaries and authorities. It is these bodies that can create the appropriate legal environment, permitting arbitration users, counsel, arbitral institutions and arbitrators to fashion the largely multicultural context which will satisfy their needs and aspirations as to the settlement of business disputes. In other words, for an international commercial arbitration culture to develop, a parallel culture, favouring the autonomy of and providing support for the international commercial arbitration process, needs to be developed at the level of national jurisdictions. The evolution of an international commercial arbitration culture is then closely associated with the development of a parallel culture, shared by national jurisdictions all over the world, which minimises the interference and maximises the support of national judiciaries *vis-à-vis* international commercial arbitrations. This latter culture is also based on certain ideas, increasingly shared by national jurisdictions, regarding the facilitation of international commercial arbitration. These find expression in common patterns of legislation and case law increasingly adopted or followed in different parts of the world and which now is more and more difficult to pigeonhole in this or that country or group of countries or indeed any other pre-conceived category.

For this reason, it is of the highest importance to introduce legislation and foster the inculcation and dissemination of ideas at the level of the local judiciary, academia and legal profession, which permit the world-wide development of the international commercial arbitral process in the cultural autonomy discussed above. The result will be a process sufficiently detached from parochial local attitudes and not only free of undue local interference from national courts, but enjoying their support. This is never more so than in the developing world or in countries interested in facilitating or attracting international commercial arbitration. It may be a truism, but nonetheless a fact, that arbitration may not progress without governmental support. This means the creation of a legislative background and policies advanced by the judiciary that are conducive to facilitating the exercise of the parties' autonomy in the fashioning of their arbitral proceedings. Such a background must on one hand shield the sphere of private ordering from the interference of courts and authorities, while on the other making available the support of those local courts to permit the arbitral proceedings to continue when faced with the recalcitrance of an unwilling party. The necessary and unavoidable additional element that also has to be provided through governmental action is a satisfactory legal framework permitting the effective and swift enforcement of arbitral awards, both domestic and foreign, within the jurisdictional reach of the local enforcement structure.

II

It is precisely in this direction that recent efforts in Latin America, to create a more user-friendly environment in respect of international commercial arbitration, are oriented. It is now possible to say that, for a number of economic and sociological reasons, Latin American countries have shifted from a culture traditionally adverse to international commercial arbitration to one that regards this method of dispute resolution as an important tool for permitting the administration of a type of justice adapted to the needs of international commercial or economic disputes with the ultimate purpose of fostering economic development and investment in the region.

Such a shift from one culture to the other has been largely engineered through governmental action, began in the early 1980s as part of a more general response to the economic and social crisis shaking most of Latin America. That crisis showed that the economic and productive structures in the region were not adequate for coping with the challenges posed by economic and technological change in the world and the needs of a growing population. The countries of Latin America, at the initiative of their governments, but also with the wide approval of both business, academic and professional circles, became involved in the process of shifting from policies and a culture traditionally adverse to alternative means of dispute resolution, particularly where international commercial arbitration was involved, to policies and a culture advancing such methods.[2] This was in the context of general policies at domestic and international levels, aimed at privatising the public sector, favouring free market access to foreign business and investment, and reducing or eliminating tariff and other barriers to trade. The regional economic co-operation and integration systems were also redesigned in tune with concepts of open regionalism, as opposed to nationalism, aiming at the integration of national territories in the international globalised economies and minilateral and multilateral schemes were set up to that end.

It should not be thought, however, that international and domestic commercial arbitration was unknown or that it was not contemplated in the local legislation. By the 1930s, there was hardly a procedural, civil or commercial code in Latin America that did not include provisions on arbitration. It is also true that business circles in Latin America always showed sympathy towards this method of dispute resolution as evidenced by initiatives from the chambers of commerce of countries such as Argentina, Colombia, Peru or Mexico to promote arbitration. Many of these institutions set up permanent arbitration boards, as in the case of the Buenos Aires Stock Exchange in Argentina, or introduced rules for administering arbitrations, as in the case of the Buenos Aires, Lima or Bogota Chambers of Commerce.

Nevertheless, the attitude of the governments and judiciary, and indeed important sections of the legal profession was not always so positive. Furthermore, most of the Codes, which reflected the ideas regarding arbitration at the end of the 19th century or during the first decades of the 20th century, when they were adopted, had long since become

[2] In general, H. Grigera Naón, 'Arbitration in Latin America: Overcoming Traditional Hostility (An Update)' in (1991) 22 *University of Miami Inter-American Law Review* 203.

antiquated. In short, the openness regarding arbitration, particularly present in many Latin American business circles, was often not matched by government policies. These were frequently aimed at neither facilitating arbitration abroad between nationals or residents and foreign parties, nor the recognition or enforcement of foreign arbitral awards, nor by legislative change. Two additional factors were the traditional Latin American objections to the recognition of arbitration in respect of vital economic matters affecting national sovereignty, such as natural resources or foreign investment, and the stagnation of the local economies, and hence cross-border commercial exchanges. (The latter was due in part to the adoption of protectionist policies regarding foreign trade and investment.) These inevitably led to the non-arbitrability of many disputes of an economic or business nature and had the effect of discouraging commercial arbitration, particularly in connection with international transactions.

III

But, as indicated, this cultural opposition to commercial arbitration in Latin America is in the process of fading away, due partly to a shift in government policies and attitudes but also in response to other social factors, such as the growing awareness of the advantages of international commercial arbitration. This has come about through education and exposure to foreign ideas, often the result of travelling, studying abroad and telecommunications as well as the knowledge of foreign languages. All of these were simply not as easily available to previous generations of lawyers, government officials and academicians as they are today.

This cultural shift has led, or is in the process of leading, to two phenomena: (i) the change in local or national arbitration legislation; and (ii) the ratification of international agreements favouring arbitration.

The first has found expression mainly in two different ways: (a) through the adoption of UNCITRAL's Model Law by following in principle its provisions with little or no change; and (b) by introducing changes to existing legislation in response to historical needs which, although they had been identified (as had their solutions) years or even decades before, had not been addressed to any degree. There was also the direct or indirect influence of the UNCITRAL Model Law, the institutional arbitration rules and the rules commonly administered at the time.

As an example of (a), reference should be first made to Mexico's adoption of the Model Law for both domestic and international arbitrations. This was almost verbatim with only a few changes, such as that providing for the applicable law to be determined by the arbitral tribunal.[3] A similar approach, albeit with some minor differences, has been followed by the new Arbitration Act of Guatemala, which applies to both national and international arbitration.[4]

Special mention should also be made of the new Peruvian General Arbitration Act of January 1996.[5] It is divided into two parts, one concerning domestic arbitration, and the other international. The part on international arbitration clearly follows the pattern and principles of the Model Law. That on domestic arbitration is also influenced to a certain extent by ideas inspired by the Model Law. The Act, however, not only covers commercial arbitration, but refers to all types, commercial or otherwise, provided that the subject-matter of the dispute is susceptible to settlement by arbitration, i.e., that all matters that may be settled by the parties are arbitrable. It is interesting to note that the provisions regarding international arbitration, although in essence follow, and even mirror, the provisions of the Model Law, still differ from it in relation to a number of important matters.

For example, where an objection is made to an arbitrator on grounds of prejudice, the decision taken by the arbitral tribunal or institution is final and binding and hence may not be appealed before the national courts. This is without prejudice to the court's jurisdiction to hear an attack on the final award on the basis of lack of independence or impartiality of the arbitrator.[6] A similar principle applies when the arbitral tribunal's jurisdiction has been questioned but refuses to declare itself incompetent: no recourse against such a decision is possible, although

3 See J. Trevino, 'International Commercial Arbitration in Mexico' in (1997) *The ICC International Court of Arbitration Bulletin*, Special Supplement on International Commercial Arbitration in Latin America 54 (Latin American Supplement).

4 M. Ibarguen S., 'Arbitration in Guatemala' in (1997) *Latin American Supplement* 45.

5 Ley General de Arbitraje No. 26572, El Peruano, 5 January 1996 (Peruvian Law). See U. Montoya A., 'Arbitration in Peru' in (1997) *Latin American Supplement* 74; F. Cantuarias S., *Nueva Ley General de Arbitraje Peruana -Ley 26572-, No. 5998* Jurisprudencia Argentina, Advanced Sheet of 14 August 1996, 9.

6 Art. 31, Peruvian Law.

the lack of jurisdiction may be invoked in order to have the final award set aside.[7] The mere existence of an arbitration agreement will suffice to obtain a court order staying court proceedings in respect of a dispute to which it is subject, save in exceptional cases, for example where the arbitral agreement is manifestly null, void or inoperative under the governing law chosen by the parties, the relevant dispute falls under the exclusive jurisdiction of Peruvian courts, or the arbitral agreement is contrary to the forum's principles of public policy (*ordre public international*).[8] Like the Swiss international arbitration statute,[9] if an international arbitration is to take place in Peru but none of the parties is a national or a resident of Peru, they may contract out, in full or in part, of the means for setting aside contemplated by the Act. In this respect, the Act follows the Model Law, with, however, the proviso that the ensuing award may not be enforced in Peru other than by means of the controls and procedures reserved for the enforcement of foreign awards or awards rendered abroad.[10] In the absence of an exclusion agreement, and in contrast to the Model Law, awards under international arbitrations rendered in Peru may only be set aside by those means provided for in the Act. Their enforcement, however, may not be opposed on similar grounds to those pertaining to the enforcement of awards rendered outside Peru if they have not been set aside before the time limit for filing such an application has elapsed.[11] However, in Peru, as probably in any Latin American country, if the court finds that an award, though made in Peru, infringes fundamental principles of public policy, it may refuse to enforce it, even though no means of recourse has either been filed against the award or is even pending.

An example of (b) is the recent Brazilian law of 23 September 1996.[12] Brazil is particularly noteworthy, since before the new legislation it was the last South American country (after the change in the law in Venezuela

[7] Art. 39, Peruvian Law.

[8] Art. 99, Peruvian Law.

[9] Art. 192, Switzerland's 1987 Private International Law Statute.

[10] Art. 126, Peruvian Law.

[11] Arts. 125, 127–129, Peruvian Law. See H. Grigera Naón, *Arbitraje Comercial Internacional en el Mundo Actual*, No. 5998 Jurisprudencia Argentina, Advanced Sheet of 14 August 1996, 31, 36–37.

[12] 'Brazilian Law'. See C. Nehring Netto, 'The New Brazilian Arbitration Law' in (1997) *Latin American Supplement* 11.

in 1986)[13] where specific performance of an arbitration agreement was not available. An arbitration agreement may now be enforced in Brazil through the courts where the attitude or conduct of either party is recalcitrant, since the new legislation now allows for specific performance to enforce the arbitration agreement.[14] In fact, the prevailing view in the specialist literature is that if, after an actual dispute has arisen, the arbitration agreement sufficiently determines the means to initiate arbitral proceedings, either directly or indirectly, by referring to specific institutional arbitration rules, the new law does not require the additional execution of a *compromiso* to give effect to it.[15] In other words, the *compromiso* is not required if the arbitration agreement provides that the arbitration shall be conducted according to specific institutional arbitration rules. It is certainly hoped that the Brazilian courts will follow this interpretation, since, under the new law, if the arbitrator designated in a *compromiso* dies or cannot perform his functions, the document will cease to be effective unless the parties expressly agree on the person to replace him.[16]

As a result of the new legislation, the principles of autonomy of the arbitration agreement and of the *kompetenz-kompetenz* of the arbitrators are now expressly recognised.[17] In addition, arbitrators are authorised to decide disputes by applying *lex mercatoria* (general principles of law, usages, customs and rules of international commerce).[18]

The new law has also significantly improved the legal framework regarding the recognition and enforcement of foreign arbitral awards in Brazil. Grounds for recognition and enforcement introduced by the new legislation follow the New York Convention very closely.[19] The obsolete

13 See Codigo de Procedimiento Civil de Venezuela, Gaceta Oficial de la Republica de Venezuela, No. 4196 Extraordinario of 2 August 1990 ('Venezuelan Law') and J. Rodner, 'Arbitration in Venezuela' in (1997) *Latin American Supplement* 90.

14 Art. 7, Brazilian Law.

15 Arts. 5–6, Brazilian Law. See P. Pinheiro Carneiro, *Aspectos Procesuais da Nova Lei de Arbitragem*, in Arbitragem, a nova lei brasileira (9307 /96) e a praxe internacional (P. Borba Casella, Coordenador) 131, 132–135 (1997); M. Basso, *LEI Nova Revitaliza a Arbitragem no Brasil como Metodo Alternativo-Extrajudicial de Solucao de Conflitos de Interesses*, 85 RT: Fasc.Civ. 11,16/19 (1996). However, see A. Pucci, *Arbitragem Comercial nos Paises do Mercosul* 99 (1997).

16 Art. 12, Brazilian Law.

17 Art. 8, Brazilian Law.

18 Art. 2, Brazilian Law.

19 Art. 38, Brazilian Law.

requirement that a foreign award may not be submitted for confirmation by the Brazilian Supreme Court without having previously been confirmed (and in practice transformed into a court decision) in the country where it was rendered has been abolished.[20] The same applies to the provision that an award rendered abroad could only be enforced in Brazil if notification of the arbitral request to the Brazilian party (i.e. party resident or domiciled in Brazil) had been made according to the rules applicable to court proceedings in Brazil. Under the new law, service of process on a Brazilian resident or domiciliary is valid if executed according to the rules of procedure governing the arbitration. Accordingly, notification of the arbitral proceedings is now possible by mail.[21]

As for (ii), in Latin America, as in other regions of the world, the first advances towards international commercial arbitration as a favoured means of resolving disputes were made through the ratification of international conventions. These predated, sometimes by many years, the streamlining of national laws on arbitration and facilitated the recognition and enforcement of arbitral awards and other issues relating to the effectiveness of arbitral agreements and the conduct of arbitral proceedings. In fact, South American efforts in this area go back to the Montevideo Treaties of 1889 and 1940 regarding the recognition and enforcement of court decisions and arbitral awards and the Bustamante Code of 1928, still applicable in some South American and Caribbean countries, which also contains provisions in this area. Though these are long since outdated and contain requirements for the recognition and enforcement of arbitral awards which would not meet standards now generally accepted, they clearly show the early interest in Latin America for arbitration as a method for the settlement of international commercial disputes.

In keeping with such tradition, the new cultural trend in the region in favour of international commercial arbitration also reveals itself through the general ratification by Latin American countries of the 1958 New York Convention – Brazil being perhaps the one significant exception. But Brazil, like not only most other Latin American countries but also the US, has ratified the 1975 Panama Inter-American Convention on International Commercial Arbitration.[22] This Convention reproduces almost verbatim article V of the New York Convention regarding the recognition and enforcement of foreign arbitral awards. In addition,

[20] Arts. 34–35, Brazilian Law.
[21] Art. 39, Brazilian Law.
[22] See English text in (1997) *Latin American Supplement* 11.

article 3 of the Inter-American Convention incorporates a very interesting feature. If the parties have not agreed on the applicable procedural law, arbitral proceedings shall be governed by the rules of procedure of the Inter-American Arbitration Commission. These rules follow very closely the UNCITRAL Arbitration Rules. The text is currently interpreted as meaning that if the parties remain silent, although the seat of the international commercial arbitration is located in a member country whose legislation on arbitration is obsolete, it shall be superseded by the rules of procedure of the Inter-American Arbitration Commission. These incorporate, *inter alia*, principles such as the autonomy of the arbitration agreement, the *Kompetenz-Kompetenz* of arbitrators, empowerment of arbitrators to grant or issue interim measures of protection, and do not require a special submission or *compromiso* to be signed after the dispute has arisen. These rules apply irrespective of any provisions to the contrary that appear in otherwise applicable domestic law and procedure, except for those of mandatory or public policy nature.[23] This Convention also permits international commercial arbitration panels to be composed of persons who are not necessarily nationals of the country where the arbitration takes place and thus in this respect supersedes the parochial requirements of certain national jurisdictions.

Other major developments evidencing the change of Latin American culture regarding international commercial arbitration is the general abandoning of positions close to the Calvo Doctrine. This doctrine, which covers matters as diverse as foreign investment, ownership of real estate or exploitation of natural resources, rules out any agreement concerning the arbitration's forum or procedure that denies jurisdiction to the courts of the host country. It applies even where the transaction could be considered as having international contacts or elements. Such developments have been expressed through (i) the modification of national laws, constitutions and international agreements (e.g., Peruvian domestic law or Andean Pact regional law), to render arbitrable, *inter alia*, transactions to which the state, a state entity or instrumentality is a party,

23 Art. 1(2) of the rules of procedure of the Inter-American Commercial Arbitration Commission provide that they shall not apply if they conflict with a provision of the law applicable to the arbitration, from which the parties cannot derogate. Current efforts to modify art. 1(2) are aimed at making clear that this would only happen if such mandatory provisions embody principles of natural justice or *ordre public international*.

technology transfer transactions, or transactions relating to the exploitation of natural resources; and (ii) the signing of bilateral investment treaties and multilateral economic co-operation agreements covering, *inter alia*, protection of foreign investments (e.g., NAFTA, Group of Three Treaty, MERCOSUR's Colonia and Buenos Aires Protocols or ICSID), all of which permit the private investor to resort to international arbitration to seek redress for grievances resulting from violations of standards of protection defined or referred to in such agreements.[24]

In short, as far as the legal framework is concerned, the new culture has led, in Latin America as in other parts of the world, to the elimination of the restrictions that prevented the parties from agreeing on arbitration abroad in the case of international transactions or which hindered the arbitrability of certain disputes (e.g. those relating to foreign investment, technology transfers, or natural resources) or the capacity of the state itself to be a party to arbitration. Also, through case law, new legislation or the ratification of international conventions, certain aspects of domestic procedural law normally not perceived as user-friendly or suited to the needs of international commercial arbitration (e.g., *compromiso*, lack of legal autonomy of the arbitral agreement, arbitrators' incapacity to decide on their own jurisdiction, exclusion of foreigners from arbitral panels, etc.) have in some cases been abolished completely and in others ruled inapplicable to international commercial arbitrations.

The evolution, however, of national laws and court decisions towards standards more adapted to the needs of international commercial arbitration is still in progress in Latin America, as indeed in other parts of the world traditionally considered more open to arbitration.

Even today, in countries like Argentina or Chile, the setting up of an arbitral tribunal, including the arbitrators' power to accept jurisdiction, is very much a matter for the courts. The submission or *compromiso*, a document setting out, among other things, a description of the parties' claims and the issues to be settled through arbitration, is still required and must be placed before the court at the court's behest if one of the parties refuses to go to arbitration. In these countries, even if there is an arbitration agreement, the *compromiso* is to be executed once the dispute

[24] H. Grigera Naón, *Paises de America Latina como Sede de Arbitrajes Comerciales Internacionales*, Boletin de la Corte Internacional de Arbitraje de la CCI, El Arbitraje Comercial Internacional, Suplemento Especial, 47 (1995).

to be submitted to arbitration has arisen.[25] Until very recently, Venezuela did not authorise the specific performance of arbitration agreements. Before the change in the law in 1986,[26] the only means of enforcing an arbitration agreement against a party who refused to comply with it was either to file a claim for compensation or damages for breach of the arbitration agreement or to enforce a penalty clause, inserted in the agreement, that provided for pecuniary sanctions for breach.

Under the present legislation for non-commercial arbitrators in Venezuela, however, even where the parties are in agreement, both that arbitration should commence and on who the arbitrators should be, the arbitrators must be appointed by the courts through a judicial hearing.[27] The new Venezuelan Arbitration Law[28] applying to commercial arbitrations only (art. 1) does not require the constitution of the arbitral panel with the intervention of the courts when the dispute is submitted to institutional arbitration (arts. 11–14). In the case of 'independent' arbitrations, or commercial arbitrations not conducted under procedural rules previously agreed by the parties (art. 15), the situation is not so clear. Since the provisions for non-commercial arbitrations subsidiarily apply to matters relating to commercial arbitrations,[29] it could be argued that the constitution of an arbitral panel in an independent commercial arbitration must be made through a court hearing as required by article 608 of the Venezuelan Civil Code of Procedure. In some Latin American countries, such as Chile, such basic principles as the force of the arbitration agreement to govern the underlying transaction and the power of arbitrators to decide on their own jurisdiction do not receive clear recognition in the local procedural codes. They are thus at best confirmed by a long and continuous sequence of judicial precedents. In others, such as Argentina[30] or Brazil,[31] disagreements as to the arbitrability of the dispute are preliminary matters to be decided by a court of law. If the issue is raised, arbitral proceedings are suspended until a final decision on the

[25] For instance, Arg. arts. 739–742 of the National Code of Civil Procedure.
[26] But now, see art. 609 Venezuelan Law.
[27] Art. 608, Venezuelan Law.
[28] Venezuela, *Ley de Arbitraje Comercial,* Gaceta Oficial de la Republica de Venezuela, No. 36, 7 April 1998.
[29] See A. Baumeister Toledo, 'Algunas consideraciones sobre el procedimiento aplicable en los casos de arbitrajes regidos por la Ley de Arbitraje Comercial in (1999) *Seminario sobre la Ley de Arbitrage Comercial,* Caracas, 63, 67–70.
[30] Arg. art. 752 of the National Code of Civil Procedure.
[31] Art. 25, Brazilian Law.

arbitrability of the dispute has been taken by the domestic court. In the case of Brazil, the suspension is, however, interpreted as not being absolute since the arbitral tribunal will still be able to hear witnesses and adopt urgent procedural measures.[32]

Nevertheless, such throwbacks from the past do not significantly detract from the overwhelming trend favouring commercial arbitration in Latin America nor from the positive disposition of Latin American parties to resort to international commercial arbitration for the resolution of business disputes. Generally, it may be said that reasons prompting Latin American parties to opt for this do not differ substantially from those in other parts of the world.

Latin American parties seek international commercial arbitration, not in order to evade prohibitions that exist under a particular national law, but because of its neutrality in respect of any particular national legal system and its detachment from local or national bias. The idea seems largely to have been abandoned that the choice of a foreign law to govern the matter in dispute and for it to be heard in a foreign forum or in international or 'foreign' commercial arbitration merely serves the purpose of evading national public policy or the legal requirements of a particular forum. Rather, parties resort to international commercial arbitration because they realise that the non-Latin American party will not accept the matter being adjudicated before Latin American courts. Nor will the Latin American party be comfortable at being compelled to litigate before the national courts of the other party, under a court procedure unfamiliar to his usual counsel and thus which requires a foreign local counsel whom he does not normally use or trust.

In this context, concerns as to the cost of the arbitration, though of course always relevant, are not necessarily decisive. Provided that the means to resolve the dispute is international commercial arbitration and that acceptable conditions of neutrality are fulfilled, Latin American parties are willing to arbitrate in a more or less de-nationalised context, whether in their own country or abroad. That said, cost considerations (for instance travel expenses) may of course make it more attractive for a Latin American party to arbitrate in his own country rather than abroad. Nevertheless, it is not unusual to see arbitrations, where both parties are Latin American, being conducted or located, by agreement between the parties, in a third country of Latin America, or even elsewhere. It also

[32] See P. Pinheiro Carneiro, *supra* n. 15, at 146.

happens that parties from the same Latin American country seek commercial arbitration in a third country, whether in Latin America or not, even where the dispute is a domestic one. Alternatively, they may agree to the dispute being arbitrated in their own country but under the rules of an international arbitration institution which is not based there. In both instances, parties normally do so to avoid unnecessary interference or supervision from the courts of a specific country or to enhance the atmosphere of neutrality surrounding the resolution of the dispute, free from parochial local issues or the influence of local procedural law on the arbitration. They may also find it convenient on account of the specific character of the applicable law, the language of the contract and the expertise required to resolve the dispute. Consider, for example, a dispute relating to an oil and gas joint venture agreement, drafted in English in accordance with standard industry terms, governed by the law of a US oil state and requiring an expert interpretation of the usages and practices internationally recognised in the oil industry.

Such a cultural shift does not mean that Latin American countries are adopting a new arbitration culture characteristic of Latin America. On the contrary, Latin America is incorporating what is increasingly the predominant world-wide arbitration culture, which has certain basic features common to jurisdictions in all continents, from the US, England and France to Singapore, Hong Kong and Australia. It is addressed to a business community made up of the operators of international commerce, public or private alike, who seek a specific product. This product may be defined as a case management system, not administered by the state, that is capable of delivering to the user or customer, in an efficient, expeditious and cost effective way, a fair resolution of the dispute under conditions of neutrality. That neutrality relates to the cultural approach to dispute resolution, the choice of the adjudicators, the conduct of the proceedings and the decision-making process.[33]

IV

One feature of this new phenomenon, apparent in the new trends in Latin America favouring international commercial arbitration, is the clear

[33] See M. Mustill, International Arbitration Conference, Boston, MA, US, September 1996 'A Commercial Way to Justice' (1997) 63 *Arbitration* 15.

sympathy, and even preference, for forms of administered or institutional, rather than *ad hoc* arbitration.

This phenomenon is apparent at different levels. One example, already mentioned, is the fact that the 1975 Inter-American Convention on International Commercial Arbitration refers to the rules of the Inter-American Arbitration Commission as the ones to apply to international commercial arbitrations in the absence of any decision by the parties to the contrary. Another example is the reference in Latin American arbitration laws to the application of the rules of institutional arbitration as an alternative to the arbitration norms contained in the national codes of procedure. As already indicated, in the case of Brazil, such a reference would imply that a *compromiso* would no longer be required as an additional formality.[34] A striking example is the General Arbitration Law of Peru. This provides that, where an objection is lodged against given arbitrators, the arbitral institution's decision on the matter is final and binding and may not be reviewed by national courts.[35] Further, the Peruvian state and its bodies, entities, agencies or organs may only submit the resolution of their international commercial disputes to reputable arbitral institutions.[36] In the case of ICC arbitration, it should be noted, among other examples, that bilateral international co-operation agreements entered into by the Republic of Cuba with other countries, such as Spain, provide for ICC arbitration as one of the options offered to the foreign investor for the resolution of investment disputes between the private investor and the host state.[37] ICC arbitration is also, under the Act of the Venezuelan Congress of 4 July 1995, the arbitral mechanism for the resolution of disputes contemplated in the General Conditions for Contracting between the state-controlled Petroleos de Venezuela SA (PEDEVESA) or its affiliates and private contractors – domestic or foreign – for the exploration in search of hydrocarbons in Venezuela.[38]

34 See *supra* n. 15 and corresponding text.
35 See *supra*, n. 6 and corresponding text.
36 Art. 92, Peruvian Law.
37 Cuba Y Reino de España, Convenio de Promocion y Proteccion Reciproca de Inversiones, Official Gazette of 18 November 1995, No. 276.
38 Venezuela, General Conditions for joint venture agreements for the exploration and exploitaition of hydrocarbons, Official Gazette of the Republic of Venezuela, No. 35754 of 17 July 1995.

At the level of Latin American users, international commercial arbitration cases rarely appear to be submitted to *ad hoc*, rather than administered or institutional, forms of arbitration.

There are certainly historical, as well as practical, reasons for this preference. On the one hand, commercial arbitration in Latin America, even when it did not enjoy a good reputation in governmental, legal profession and academic circles, has traditionally advanced and developed through institutions representing or advocating the interests of business circles which in turn introduced arbitration rules administered by those institutions. Often, such institutions also provided facilities in which arbitrations could be held, made available lists of arbitrators to the interested parties, or even offered to the users permanent arbitration tribunals deciding cases in accordance with the institution's rules. In this context, an agreement should not be forgotten between business institutions in Argentina and the United States of America of 1916 (the Agreement) and its attached arbitration rules (the Rules) and rules on disposal of goods.[39] This set up a system of administered commercial arbitration for resolving business disputes, mainly arising out of international contracts for the sale of goods between nationals of those countries. Not only does it constitute the first precedent for a co-ordinated international commercial arbitration facility in the Americas, but it was also the direct inspiration for the arbitration rules adopted in 1923 by the Council of the International Chamber of Commerce, headquartered in Paris, and the establishment of what is now the International Court of Arbitration of the International Chamber of Commerce.[40]

[39] See Convenio de Arbitraje Comercial entre la Bolsa de Comercio de Buenos Aires y la Camara de Comercio de los Estados Unidos de America y Reglamentos Incorporados al Mismo in 575 Boletin Oficial de la Bolsa de Comercio de Buenos Aires, 17 April 1916, at 9 *et seq.* My special thanks to Jorge Bacque, former Justice at the Supreme Court of Argentina and former member of the Permanent Arbitration Tribunal of the Buenos Aires Stock Exchange for providing me with copies of this document.

[40] Eric Schwartz, my predecessor as Secretary General of the International Court of Arbitration of the International Chamber of Commerce, was the first to unearth this important precedent. See E. Schwartz, 'The Practices and Experiences of the ICC Court, in Conservatory and Provisional Measures in International Arbitration' in (1993) *ICC Publication* 519 at 45, n. 1. As indicated by Mr. Schwartz, a memorandum from Mr. Roberto Pozzi, included in brochure No. 13 published by the Council of the International Chamber of Commerce in 1920 under the title 'Proposed Plan for ICC Arbitration' demonstrates the direct links between the first ICC arbitration rules of 1923 and the Agreement.

It is worth spending some time on the analysis of the Agreement and the Rules, since they illustrate that international commercial arbitration always results from efforts based on a multicultural and multinational approach regarding dispute resolution. These are now more broadly echoed by the prevailing conceptions of international commercial arbitration in Latin America and also constitute characteristic features of the modern international commercial process. The Agreement is also evidence that international commercial arbitration is based on the creation of a micro-cultural environment for the resolution of investment disputes. Such an environment is shielded from the particularities of national laws and procedures and the unilateral perspective for resolving disputes which would result from considering them from the angle of a specific legal culture.

The Agreement started by establishing that both organisations would exert their influence on Argentine and US businessmen, to persuade them to consent to arbitration under the Rules, agreed by the Buenos Aires Stock Exchange and the US Chamber of Commerce.[41] It provided that the arbitral clause may be agreed upon by cable and that the arbitration was to be held in the country in which the goods had to be delivered to the buyer.[42] This principle was strongly advocated by the Argentine side, a net importer of manufactured goods from the US, since it would permit Argentine importers to arbitrate in Argentina, without the expense of travelling to the US to arbitrate there.[43] Arbitrations held in Argentina were to be administered by the Buenos Aires Stock Exchange; those in the US by the US Chamber of Commerce.[44] Both institutions respectively had the power to appoint arbitrators should the parties have failed to do so.[45]

For the purpose of administering arbitrations, each institution created an Arbitration Committee comprised of five persons. Each Committee would monitor and administer arbitrations taking place under the Agreement in their respective country. In the case of the Argentine Committee, two members were appointed by the US Chamber of Commerce, subject

[41] Art. I of the Agreement.

[42] Arts. III–IV of the Agreement.

[43] Speech of Mr. Ricardo Aldao on the date of signature of the Agreement, in No. 575 Boletin Oficial de la Bolsa de Comercio de Buenos Aires, 17 April 1916 at 543.

[44] Arts. V–VI of the Agreement.

[45] *Ibid.*

to confirmation by the Buenos Aires Stock Exchange and the three remaining members by the Buenos Aires Stock Exchange, subject to confirmation by the US Chamber of Commerce.[46] The same method was followed for determining the membership of the Arbitration Committee of the US Chamber of Commerce: two of its members were appointed by the Buenos Aires Stock Exchange, subject to confirmation by the US Chamber of Commerce, while the other three were appointed by the US Chamber of Commerce subject to confirmation by the Buenos Aires Stock Exchange.[47] This shared appointment of the members of the respective national Arbitration Committees aimed at ensuring a certain cultural equilibrium in the mechanism for resolving disputes. The requirement for the consensus of both institutions for the appointment of Committee members undoubtedly placed the Committees in a good position to carry out the duties inherent in their task of 'exercising general powers for the monitoring and administration of arbitrations under the agreement and to do all the best they could for advancing arbitration as a friendly means of resolving commercial disputes'[48] within an atmosphere in which different cultural approaches would be properly represented and parochial excesses would be avoided.

Each Committee would have an official roster, comprising at least 30 persons of 'exceptional honesty and capacity' and representing as many branches of commerce as possible.[49] This suggests that the arbitrators were more likely to be merchants or businessmen than lawyers. Fifteen members of the roster of the Argentine Committee would be chosen by the US Chamber of Commerce and confirmed by the Buenos Aires Stock Exchange and 15 *vice versa*.[50] The same principle would be applied for determining membership in the roster for the US Committee.[51] This further confirms the importance given to the principle of neutrality and the existence of a multicultural environment for the resolution of disputes.

Both institutions undertook to exert all their influence to ensure the enforcement of awards rendered under this arbitration system. Upon learning that an award had not been enforced, the respective institution

46 *Ibid.*
47 *Ibid.*
48 Art. VI of the Agreement.
49 Art. VIII of the Agreement.
50 Arts. VIII–IX of the Agreement.
51 *Ibid.*

was to draw the matter to the attention of the defaulting party. If such party still did not enforce the award, the institution was to take all necessary measures to punish the defaulting party within the scope of its powers. Both participating institutions would publish, at least on a quarterly basis, a bulletin summarising awards rendered under this system, a list of awards rendered, the name of those not complying with awards and the reasons for such refusal.[52] Interestingly enough, and in accordance with trends which have now appeared in certain jurisdictions,[53] confidentiality was not one of the leading concerns. However, although members of the relevant Committee could attend hearings and the arbitration file could be consulted at all times by the parties, and even by third parties with the Committee's written authorisation, arbitral proceedings would not be in principle rendered public without the consent of the parties.[54] The Committees were entitled, after informing the parties, to adopt interim measures of protection affecting the subject matter of the dispute (i.e. the goods), aimed at 'avoiding increased losses' or for selling goods. Proceeds obtained from such sales were to be deposited in banks until the end of the arbitration.[55]

In addition, for arbitrations conducted under this system, each institution adopted the Rules governing them in respect of the production of evidence, hearings and the payment of arbitration costs and arbitral fees.[56] Arbitral decisions would be taken *ex aequo et bono* with the least possible loss of 'time, energy and money and causing as little irritation as possible'.[57] Nothing should be taken to preclude the appointment of a sole arbitrator.[58] Awards were notified to the parties by the president of the Arbitration Committee of the country in which the arbitration took place.[59]

52 Arts. X–XI of the Agreement.
53 See J. Paulsson and N. Rawding, 'The Trouble with Confidentiality' in (1994) 5 *ICC International Court of Arbitration Bulletin* 1 at 48.
54 Art. III of the Rules.
55 Art. XII of the Agreement and Rules on the Disposal of Goods, which may be also found in No. 575 Boletin Oficial de la Bolsa de Comercio de Buenos Aires, 17 April 1916 at 536 *et seq*.
56 Art. XIII of the Agreement.
57 Art. VI of the Rules.
58 Art. VII of the Rules.
59 Art. XIII of the Rules.

V

Though the ICC arbitration system as it exists today has its own characteristics which clearly differentiate it from the Americas' 1916 model, it has maintained and further developed the multicultural and multinational approach that underlie its initial sources. Because the ICC arbitration rules have invariably maintained, despite the inevitable updatings required by the passing of time, specific features in keeping with those basic multicultural and multinational traditions, it is today in an excellent position to satisfy the needs and expectations of both the Latin American party and the non-Latin American party doing business in Latin America or with a Latin American party. Their disputes can therefore be adjudicated within the context of a case management system of proven efficiency, which allows for the fashioning of arbitral proceedings flexible enough to adapt themselves to the specific micro-cultural characteristics of the specific arbitration at stake. It may be said without exaggeration that the ICC arbitration system is now the only one that is truly global and universal in its organisation and scope. In 1996, for the first time since the creation of the ICC arbitration system in 1923, less than 50 per cent of the parties to cases filed in a given year were from Western Europe. A substantial increase in the participation in ICC arbitrations of parties from other parts of the world, such as North America, Central and Eastern Europe, Asia and Latin America has become a current and established trend in recent years.

The increase in the percentage of Latin American parties in ICC arbitration eloquently illustrates this. In 1996, cases involving Latin American and Caribbean parties represented 11 per cent of the total filed with the ICC in that year,[60] an increase of about 4 per cent on the previous year[61] and more than double the percentage of cases involving parties from this area five years before.

ICC arbitrations may take place in any part of the world, a feature that has been tested again and again throughout 74 years of experience. The body in charge of administering ICC arbitrations, the ICC International Court of Arbitration, is composed of 65 members from 56 countries in all corners of both the developed and the developing world

[60] See (May 1997) *ICC International Court of Arbitration Bulletin* 7 at 8.
[61] See (May 1996) *ICC International Court of Arbitration Bulletin* 5 at 7.

and represents all the world's major legal systems. The Court's Secretariat, which assists it in the performance of its functions, is equally multinational. All of this emphasises the multicultural traits of the ICC arbitration system and guarantees the evenhanded administration of ICC arbitrations, free from cultural or other bias.

In addition, the ICC has over 65 National Committees all over the world. Court members are proposed by the respective National Committee and appointed by the Council of the International Chamber of Commerce. Where a party fails to designate an arbitrator, or when there is no agreement between the parties on the sole arbitrator or the chairman of the tribunal, it will be for the Court (other than in certain exceptional circumstances) to invite a National Committee to propose a name to the Court. The Court will normally appoint such a person unless it finds he is not independent from the parties or otherwise lacks the required ability or would not be sufficiently available throughout the arbitral proceedings to discharge his duties.

Consequently, the combined intervention of Court, National Committees and Secretariat is another guarantee, on one hand, of the cultural equanimity with which the choice of arbitrators is made and, on the other, that the choice of arbitrators is made after the cultural realities involved in the dispute have been assessed. A properly balanced panel, in the light of the origin and background of the parties and the nature and location of the dispute, is thus assured. The Court may only confirm arbitrators proposed by one or both parties, or appoint arbitrators (normally on the basis of the proposal of a national committee) if that arbitrator is independent. In other words, the arbitrator must, objectively, have no connection or relationship with either of the parties (including the party who appointed him) or their counsel that might lead to the belief that he will not carry out his duties in an unbiased or impartial manner. The fact that this evaluation is also made from the multicultural perspective of the Court is another guarantee of the evenhandedness with which arbitral independence will be considered in the process of making appointments or confirmations.

Such cultural neutrality is also decisive where the parties have failed to determine the place of the arbitration. Under the ICC arbitration rules, in the absence of stipulation by the parties, this shall be determined by the Court. The Court will do so after careful consideration of the different essential aspects of the case, in order to ensure that the venue is neutral. It may not be in the country of any of the parties to the dispute, nor may any of the parties be unduly inconvenienced by the arbitration taking place there. Such factors are considered such as the distance of the location and also take into account the general conditions there, including communications and hearing facilities and the location of or access to witnesses and other evidence. But the Court's choice also involves other considerations, such as the legal environment regarding arbitration in the possible venues and the likelihood that an award made or considered as made in such countries may be easily enforced, either in the country or abroad. The fact that the analysis of all these vital factors is made from the multicultural standpoint of the Court and its Secretariat, which combine the knowledge of different legal systems and national environments, is an additional guarantee that the chosen venue shall be properly adapted to the circumstances of the dispute.

Of course, the multicultural background of the Court plays an essential role when it comes to the scrutiny of ICC awards, one of the unique features of the ICC arbitration system. Under the ICC Rules, the Court examines the draft awards prepared by the arbitrators before they are dated and signed. Once the award has been approved by the Court (after having been scrutinised), it will be dated and signed by the arbitrators and communicated to the parties by the Secretariat. Observations of the Court as to form are binding on the arbitrators. In addition, the Court may draw the attention of the arbitrators to matters related to the merits of the dispute. These remarks, however, are not binding on the arbitrators and do not compromise their freedom to decide the dispute. The scrutiny process is aimed at identifying flaws in the awards that may adversely affect their recognition or enforcement before national jurisdictions and in practice also operates as a quality control of the final product of the arbitral tribunal. Once more, the experience and knowledge of Court members of the characteristics of different legal systems and jurisdictions and in different areas of business and economic law, as well as the Court's general multicultural background, lead to a scrutiny process based on a broad and informed debate on different aspects of the award at stake. Experience shows that the scrutiny of ICC awards by the Court is one of the reasons for their effectiveness, even where they have been challenged or their enforcement has been resisted before national courts. Last but not least, the reputation and popularity of the ICC arbitration system among users all over the world may be explained to a considerable extent by the efficient work performed by the Court throughout its history in scrutinising awards from all over the world.

On 8 April 1997, the Council of the International Chamber of Commerce adopted new, modified ICC Arbitration Rules, which came into effect on 1 January 1998. The new Rules maintain the basic features of the ICC arbitration system described above, including its universality and its multicultural and multinational approach to arbitral adjudication. At the same time, however, they aimed at making the ICC's arbitral case management more flexible, agile and efficient by incorporating a number of new provisions. These are largely inspired by the experience gathered by the ICC Court and its Secretariat over the last 20 years as well as suggestions from users of ICC arbitration and also developments observed in the case law of different jurisdictions or in comparative arbitration law. The new ICC Rules apply to arbitrations commenced on or after 1 January 1998 unless the parties agree that the ICC Rules in effect on the date of the arbitration agreement shall apply.[62]

Among the innovations aimed at making the ICC arbitration system more expeditious and user-friendly are the following:

(a) Under the old rules, terms of reference had to list the disputed issues to be decided by the arbitral tribunal. Under the new rules, these issues are to be listed unless the arbitrators judge it inappropriate to do so.[63] Consequently, the new rules permit arbitrators not to list the issues to be decided where these are sufficiently identified by the parties in the briefs or submissions exchanged before the drafting of the terms of reference. Thus, it is left to the wisdom of the arbitrators to avoid an unnecessary exercise which could lend itself to a manoeuvre in bad faith by a party seeking to use the process of identifying and describing the issues in dispute to obstruct or delay the course of the entire arbitration.

(b) Under the old rules, the arbitral tribunal could not decide on claims not contained in the terms of reference unless they were incorporated into an addendum accepted by the parties, which had to be communicated to the Court. Under the new rules, no addendum is required and no communication to the Court is needed, since it is up to the arbitral tribunal to decide, after hearing the parties, whether the new claims may be filed, taking into account when they were introduced

[62] Art. 6(1), 1998 ICC Rules.
[63] Art. 18(1)(d), 1998 ICC Rules.

and whether or not their consideration would disrupt the course of the arbitral proceedings.[64]

(c) The new rules permit the Secretary General of the Court to set the arbitration in motion by sending the file to the arbitrators once the claimant has paid the advance on costs, fixed by the Secretary General and calculated on the amount of the claim. Previously, the file could not be sent to the arbitrators without the Court having first fixed a global advance for costs, calculated on all claims and counterclaims involved in the arbitration. Under the new system, the file is sent to the arbitrators more quickly, since the global cost advance for the entire arbitration is normally fixed at a later stage.[65] The old system required 50 per cent of the global advance on costs for the entire arbitration, as fixed by the Court, to be paid in equal shares by the parties before the file could be sent to the arbitrators. This led to delays in the transmission of the file when one of the parties failed to pay its share since the arbitration could not be set in motion until the share of the defaulting or recalcitrant party had been satisfied by another party to the arbitration. Such delays are no longer possible under the new system. As an additional means of avoiding delays, the Secretary General of the Court may confirm arbitrators nominated by one of the parties, provided that they have filed an unqualified statement of independence or, if the statement is qualified, that the qualifications have not led the other party to object to the appointment of the relevant arbitrator. Should the Secretary General of the Court find that the prospective arbitrator should not be confirmed (e.g., if he considers that, in spite of the absence of qualifications in the statement of independence, the prospective arbitrator's independence is open to question), he will refer the decision whether or not he is to be confirmed to the Court.[66] The new system permits the saving of time, since normally the Secretary General will directly confirm the prospective arbitrator whose independence is unquestionable without needing to wait for a hearing of the Court. Previously, a Court ruling was required even in cases in which the potential arbitrator's independence was beyond doubt or unchallenged.

[64] Art. 19, 1998 ICC Rules.
[65] Art. 30(2), 1998 ICC Rules.
[66] Art. 9(2), 1998 ICC Rules.

(d) The new rules facilitate fast-track arbitrations by expressly permitting the parties to shorten the procedural delays contemplated in the rules, in order to expedite the arbitral proceedings. In fact, fast-track arbitrations were successfully held under the old rules with the co-operation of the ICC Court and its Secretariat.[67] The new rules also permit the Court to extend the procedural periods contemplated in the new rules, but shortened by the parties,[68] if such a reduction would jeopardise the proper exercise of the functions of the Court (e.g., the scrutiny of arbitral awards) or of the acting arbitral tribunal. Similarly, the Court may intervene if the reduction would put at risk principles of due process or the enforcement of the award (e.g. if the reduction would be such as to deny a party the possibility of being properly heard or of presenting its case).

(e) The new rules seek to promote or induce discipline by means of the organisation of the proceedings by the arbitrators in order to minimise delays. When communicating the terms of reference to the ICC Court, the arbitral tribunal is also obliged to send the parties and the ICC Court a procedural schedule or timetable[69] which may establish, *inter alia*, the chronology of hearings, production of evidence and additional memorials to be submitted by the parties. When the arbitral tribunal has come to the conclusion that the parties have had sufficient opportunity to present their respective cases, it will make an order closing the proceedings, after which no further evidence may be offered or adduced, or submissions made, without the authorisation of the tribunal. At the same time, the arbitral tribunal must communicate to the ICC Court Secretariat the date by which the award is to be made.[70]

(f) Drawing on the experience accumulated, as well as developments in comparative law and in the case law of certain countries, the new rules introduce two new provisions which have the effect of either permitting or facilitating the consideration, in one single arbitral proceeding, of claims which otherwise would require separate

67 Art. 32(1), 1998 ICC Rules.

68 Art. 32(2), 1998 ICC Rules. On past fast-track experiences under the ICC arbitration system, see articles by B. Davis, P. Nickles, D. Watkiss and H. Smit on 'ICC Fast-Track Arbitration: Different Perspectives' in (1992) 3 *ICC International Court of Arbitration Bulletin* 2 at 4–17.

69 Art. 18(4), 1998 ICC Rules.

70 Art. 22, 1998 ICC Rules.

arbitrations or of avoiding the tribunal's deliberations being paralysed as a result of the absence or lack of participation of one of its members.

The first of these concerns an arbitration involving several claimants or defendants, where they fail to agree amongst themselves on the arbitrator they are to appoint and the arbitration clause required setting up a three-member arbitral tribunal. The classic scenario is the one confronted by the French *Cour de Cassation* in the *Dutco* case.[71] The claimant named as co-defendants two different companies bound by the same arbitral clause in a joint venture agreement to which all of them were parties. However, claims made, though they arose out of the same contract, were different against each of them. The co-defendants held different positions since they were defending themselves against different claims. In addition, they did not agree on the arbitrator to be appointed on behalf of the defendants (the arbitral agreement provided for a three-member panel). The *Cour de Cassation* held that the co-defendants could not be forced, without their express consent, to accept a party arbitrator imposed on them by the intervening arbitral institution (the ICC Court). This would violate the principle of equality, since the single claimant enjoyed total freedom to designate his arbitrator, whereas the co-defendants would not be in such a position if, in the absence of an agreement, their arbitrator would be imposed on them. In such a situation, equality would only be restored if all members of the panel, including the claimant's arbitrator, were appointed by the institution. This is precisely the solution adopted by the new rules, which vest the ICC Court, unless the parties agree otherwise, with the power to appoint all three panel members in such multi-party scenarios as described above.[72]

The second provision concerns a situation in which an arbitrator has died or resigned or the ICC Court is for some other reason entitled to replace him, but for practical reasons closely associated

[71] The precise reference for the *Dutco* case is *BKMI Industrienlagen GmbH* v. *Dutco Construction Co. (Pvt.) Ltd.* No. 89-28.708Y; *Siemens AG* v. *Dutco Construction Co. (Pvt.) Ltd.* No. 89-18.726Y combined, French *Cour de Cassation,* 1ere Ch. Civile, 7 January 1992. See E. Schwartz, 'Multi-Party Arbitration and the ICC: In the Wake of *Dutco*' (1993) 10 *Journal of International Arbitration* 5.

[72] Art. 10, 1998 ICC Rules.

with the efficient and expeditious completion of arbitral proceedings, replacement is not advisable. The multiple-member arbitral panel must still give an award. Such a scenario is more likely to appear at the end of arbitral proceedings, when the tribunal has begun its deliberations prior to giving its award and a member of the tribunal refuses to participate or is prevented from doing so as a result, for instance, of a court order in his country of residence forbidding him to participate. In such a situation, removal and replacement may not be appropriate. It is likely that a substantial part of the proceedings (notably the hearings) would have to be repeated with the participation of the new arbitrator. Alternatively, the new arbitrator, appointed by the same party that designated the first one, may quite possibly use the same delaying tactics as his predecessor. In such a situation – what in the arbitral jargon is known as a 'truncated tribunal' scenario – provided that the proceedings have come to a close prior to the commencement of the tribunal's deliberations, the ICC Court, after removing the relevant arbitrator, may, if in the circumstances of the case it considers it appropriate, authorise the two remaining arbitrators to continue deliberations and make an award on their own. The Court will take such a decision only after hearing the parties and the other member of the tribunal.[73] Though this provision is seldom likely to be applied in practice, its very presence will hopefully deter disloyal or obstructionist conduct aimed at paralysing the deliberations of the arbitral panel.

(g) The new rules now include a provision permitting the arbitral tribunal to correct clerical or mathematical errors, either on its own initiative or at the request of a party, and to interpret the award at the request of a party when its meaning is not clear. Such a request by a party must be filed with the Court's Secretariat within 30 days of the date of the award. After hearing the parties, the arbitral tribunal shall have 30 days to render its decision to correct or interpret the award. That decision remains subject to the scrutiny of the ICC Court.[74]

[73] Art. 12(5), 1998 ICC Rules.
[74] Art. 29, 1998 ICC Rules.

VI

Present developments indicate that the beginning of the next millennium will see increasing demands from arbitration users to have access to forms of international commercial arbitration that are universal enough to satisfy the needs posed by the globalisation of economic relations. As current trends in Latin America reveal, these new realities mean the introduction of new players to the world of international commercial arbitration, be they businessmen, private or public entities, arbitrators or counsel. They will be anxious to learn about international commercial arbitration and to adapt or streamline national legislation, their ways of thinking and their skills in order to participate and have a say in the course of events fashioning new developments in international commercial arbitration.

More than ever before, arbitration case management systems wishing to meet the needs of this heterogeneous array of participants must maintain or enhance their multicultural approach to dispute resolution if they are to play satisfactorily the role expected of them. As its history has proved and as is constantly shown by its continuing vocation for invigorating change, the ICC business arbitration system, with its new 1998 arbitration rules, is certainly placed in an excellent position to meet these challenges.

9

Overcoming the Clash of Legal Cultures: The Role of Interactive Arbitration*

Bernardo M. Cremades

At one time, the nature of international commercial arbitration was that of a craft mastered by a small minority. As the former Secretary General of the International Chamber of Commerce's International Court of Arbitration, Frederick Eisemann, stated then, arbitration was worth as much as the arbitrators to whom it was entrusted. At that time there were only a few law firms which represented parties in arbitration proceedings, although each of them were becoming familiar with the rules of the game as they being established through a flexible, though well-consolidated, daily practice.

In contrast, today, great economic battles are fought and a true arbitration industry has emerged. It has ceased to be the activity of a few and has become a universally accepted solution for the resolution of international commercial conflicts. The number of those of us who participate today as arbitrators is extensive. Few companies, dedicated to the world of commerce, industry or international finance, have escaped participation in one way or another in international commercial arbitrations. The generalised inclusion of arbitration clauses in those contracts which they draft daily have increasingly attracted law firms from very different backgrounds and with distinct approaches to the world of arbitration. As a result, international arbitration is presently undergoing a process of harmonisation in its basic notions through a limitless combination of its different elements to achieve a pleasing effect: the adaptation of legal systems throughout the world to a global economic market and, following the innovations in telecommunications and the development of a global information infrastructure, a global society. International commercial

*This article first appeared in (1998) 14 *Arbitration International* 2 at 157.

Conflicting Legal Cultures in Commercial Arbitration, S. Frommel and B. Rider (eds), Kluwer Law International, London, 1999; ISBN 90-411-1227-8

arbitration is uniquely and inevitably undergoing this process because, historically, it is one of the earliest examples of the attempts to adapt independent national legal systems to the relentless progress of international commerce.

As a result of these developments, however, and as indicated by Professor Whitmore Gray at the conference organised in 1996 by the International Council for Commercial Arbitration in Seoul, arbitration is today a victim of its own success. Some years ago, when it was still a craft, arbitration rested in good measure within the wise discretion of arbitrators. Nowadays, new technology has made arbitration its victim. Dossiers presented to arbitral tribunals have enormously increased in volume, due to both the possibility of photocopied documents and the simplified drafting of submissions and statements through the use of sophisticated word processing programmes. It is not infrequent to find arbitrators in tribunals confused by the end of the proceedings, faced with so much argument and excessive documentation. In many instances, arbitrators must protect themselves by demanding more clarity and precision from the parties in their claims so as to identify exactly which points are at issue, whilst maintaining the right of the parties to be heard in an adversarial procedure.

The considerable participation of jurists from very different origins and with very different approaches has caused arbitral procedure to evolve in an extraordinary manner. Different geographic origins have repercussions in their respective approaches, which gives rise to an academic confrontation between those trained in the Anglo-Saxon legal profession and those having a Roman law orientation.[1] Thus, on the one hand, the Western world is

[1] It has become traditional to speak of the common law versus the civil law approach or the inquisitorial versus the adversarial approach. The essence of the adversarial procedure *(procédure contradictoire, einem kontradiktorischen Verfahren, contradittorio, proceso contradictorio*; see art. 1460.2 of the French Code of Civil Procedure art. 21.1 of the 1988 Spanish Arbitration Act: art. 182.3 of 1987 Swiss Private International Law Act (PILA)) is that, while the judge listens to the parties' evidence and arguments and decides between them, he does not make his own inquiries as to the facts, adopt conclusions of fact not proposed by either party; or propose or adopt arguments or conclusions of law differing from those which the parties put forward. These categories are convenient in the abstract because they provide ostensible common ground for lawyers who pronounce themselves of the 'civil law' or 'common law' school. Hence, the rigid application of either a common law or a civil law approach can be misleading. Fundamental to the success of such an approach is not only

traditionally characterised as a litigious culture (albeit with widely differing approaches). Indeed in Europe, we can clearly distinguish between the manner in which the practice of law is conducted on either side of the English Channel. Anglo-Saxon lawyers educated in the common law system have left their imprint, seeking to conduct arbitration proceedings in the same manner as judicial proceedings are conducted before domestic courts. In Continental Europe, the approach to the resolution of conflicts differs between areas with Germanic cultural roots and those which we may call the Latin zone of cultural influence. On the other hand, East Asian[2] and

cont.

the availability of diversity from which to choose, but also the freedom to exercise a choice so as to accede to that diversity (see *Channel Tunnel Group Limited* v. *Balfour Beatty Construction and Others* [1993] 2 WLR 262, HL). A prerequisite to the development of harmonised procedures based on the best of a diverse range of approaches is thus the freedom of the parties to choose the seat of an arbitration, the *lex arbitrii* and the applicable law. Diversity will not be preserved by national systems insisting on a parochial application of their own procedures and laws. Rather, the survival of diversity presupposes that national systems relinquish control and allow parties the freedom to go outside that system and choose their own procedures and controlling law. Otherwise, a conclusion might rapidly emerge: that these categorisations are more conducive to lazy thinking and unhelpful approximations than to a reliable conceptual framework that would help fashion a transnational *modus vivendi* out of the inconsistent patterns of national practice.

2 In his report for the 1996 ICCA Conference, Professor Yashuei Taniguchi explained the historical background of such a preference in East Asia, stating that:

> a typical example is Japan, where under the feudal regime which lasted for more than 250 years until 1868 there was no practice of law allowed to exist, there was a strong communal system to promote amicable settlement of dispute and to suppress litigation. Litigation was condemned as a moral wrongdoing to the society and to the other party. A good judge was not supposed to give a judgement but to try to give a good conciliation. This tradition was deeply embedded in the people's mind and formed a dispute resolution culture in Japan. Radical political and economic changes taking place in the past hundred years have certainly affected this culture but it still persists in many noticeable forms. In China, where this type of culture originated, a strong emphasis on the conciliation was kept even under the Maoist communists regime as the means to resolve the so-called 'contradiction within the people'. Judge's primary obligation was said to be not to decide cases but to 'educate' the parties so that they became willing to cease disputing ...

Arabic and Islamic societies[3] are known for their emphasis on conciliation.

International commercial arbitration knows of no frontiers and thus innumerable physical and legal entities, of very different nationalities and distinct cultural origins, jointly participate more and more each day in its practice. The question therefore arises whether it is appropriate to speak of arbitration as a true clash of legal cultures. It was precisely this question which led the members of the International Council for Commercial Arbitration to call the 1996 Seoul Conference, in order to discuss among professionals, from very different countries and cultural areas and in a country unfamiliar to many, the true cultural essence which underlies the practice of international commercial arbitration. At the time the conference was called, the members were all convinced that their daily practice of international commercial arbitration supposed a true clash of legal cultures. During the drafting of the papers, however, the co-ordination of so many professionals who actively participated in the conference's programme and the co-operation among all those who intervened in the meetings, cast serious doubt on the initial premise. It became ever more apparent that the harmonisation of arbitration has lead to a greater professionalism amongst those who engage in it.

Few sociological studies have been undertaken on the different legal professions and their relation to society's expectations, in particular the citizens who demand and use these services. The way in which lawyers are paid may condition their performance and how aggressively (or not) they conduct the arbitration proceedings. Where, due to ethical reasons and in order to allow access of the poor to justice, payment is based on

[3] In his report for the 1996 ICCA Conference, Ahmed Sadek El-Kosheri explained the historical background of such a selection in Arab and Islamic countries, stating that:

> Arab and Islamic societies characterised by the existence of a strong communal system to promote amicable settlement of disputes through negotiation/mediation as a first step that could lead ultimately at a later stage to conciliation/arbitration. According to the results obtained through serious anthropological studies, the region had been culturally pro-conciliation even before the appearance of Judaeo-Christian and Islamic ideals of moral harmony and peaceful settlement of disputes within the community without confrontation through litigation. This characteristic survived until the mid-20th century where 80 per cent of all disputes used to be amicably settled out of state courts by recourse to an either respected popular personality chosen for his wisdom and known integrity, either in the village rural community, within the heads of the nomadic tribe or among city merchants ...

the so-called contingency fee, an aggressive feeling is created. This probably does not exist in lawyers from countries where the so-called *de quota litis* pact is considered by law to be ethically unacceptable: a lawyer's participation in the results of a process – or the payment of his services related to those results – creates a more or less litigious society. Many of the problems which arise in practice derive fundamentally from these different ethical approaches by the lawyers from widely differing cultures.

It is difficult to define what is understood by a legal culture and even more an arbitration culture. International arbitration is a direct witness of the interaction among different legal cultures, aspects of which, as discussed below, have crystallised into formal rules or customs which consequently govern the proceedings. When arbitration becomes transnational, the cultural unity is disrupted and the resulting kaleidoscope of different cultural patterns gives rise to a multiplicity of images affecting all stages of any arbitration proceeding. Hence the need for an international arbitration culture encompassing the essentials of domestic and international philosophies. Practice tells us that overcoming the clash of legal cultures is not truly achieved through academic discussion or dogmatism, but rather through everyday practical reality. For this reason, the way to overcome the conflict of legal cultures is an increased interactive approach among those who participate in each single arbitration proceeding. In many ways, international commercial arbitration is both a paradigm of the evolution of this process of harmonisation without which the process itself could not take place. However, the unique position of international commercial arbitration at the vanguard of this process should not cause us to ignore the experience that is being gained in many other fora – regional, plurilateral or multilateral – where harmonisation is also occurring. Some of these other experiences can provide us with useful insights.[4]

Arbitrators should make a genuine effort to achieve effective communication with both the parties to the dispute and their lawyers. A prudent and experimented arbitral tribunal chairman is, without a doubt, the best instrument through which to overcome the inevitable conflicts of approach

[4] There has been recognition at an international level of the importance of the preservation of diversity to biological evolution (i.e., the Convention on Biological Diversity). The diversity of genetic materials opens the possibility of spontaneous mutation for the development of superior characteristics in organisms as well as the possibility of finding solutions to new circumstances or novel threats with which existing organisms are confronted.

which are encountered daily during arbitration proceedings. An arbitration chairman must thus possess special human and professional qualities: he should be comprehensive; he should listen carefully to the parties and should be able not only to speak their language, but also to understand their respective approaches and be acquainted with their cultural backgrounds. He must have developed, in summary, that psychological intuition appropriate for the professional experienced in the resolution of international conflicts.

There are, of course, no general rules which can be applied to establish the limits to this interactivity in the daily practice of arbitration. Experience will tell, case by case, where these limits are most appropriate. Will such interactivity eventually lead to an open discussion between the tribunal and the parties? Like so many other questions, this does not admit of a single answer. In some instances, prudence counsels the arbitral tribunal chairman not to make the slightest comment which might suggest to the parties that the matter may have been prejudged. In the majority of cases, however, once an atmosphere of understanding reigns between the parties and the arbitrators, it is logical for the tribunal to begin expressing its concerns and formulating its theories so that the parties may conduct their arguments and present their evidence in the manner desired by the tribunal.[5] There is nothing which the parties find more frustrating than receiving an arbitration award in which the arbitrators seem to have decided on arguments not made before them and which have the appearance of being the product of a private discussion of the arbitrators.

The main points concerning communication and interactivity between the tribunal and the parties are as follows: (i) the possible mediating or conciliating intervention of the arbitrators; (ii) communication between the arbitral tribunal and the parties on matters of evidence; (iii) the influence of the arbitrator's cultural background in his decision-making process; and (iv) the possible cultural friction which may arise in the collaboration between arbitrators and local state judges.

[5] Flexibility is however not free of dangers. Perhaps the greatest danger it may present is the possibility for abuse of the process by one of the parties who may wish to adopt tactics that are deliberately dilatory, obstructing the role of time limits and abusing the service of process. These are areas in which rules can provide guidance on what is expected from a party and when it is expected. However, time limits necessarily curtail flexibility. They are best contained in the Rules which lay down the procedural framework and should not be hidden in places where the parties may find themselves unwittingly trapped, since harmonisation also implies the elimination of dissonant elements.

I. 'MED-ARBITRATION'[6]

Traditionally, it was an agreed doctrine within the world of arbitration that an arbitrator's duty shall not be mixed with any mediating activity or intent to reconcile.[7] This was one of the greatest dangers widely highlighted in arbitration seminars as it was stated outright that an arbitrator who initiated conciliation or mediation was exposed to the risk of an eventual challenge. Again, the participation in international

[6] The term is an abbreviated amalgam of 'mediation-arbitration' (med-arb) to define when an attempt is first made to resolve a dispute by mutual agreement through mediation and if it fails, then directly proceeding to a binding arbitration. Med-arb is sometimes said to be superior to pure mediation on the grounds that a binding resolution is assured. It offers the following real or perceived advantages: first, that the process will, in one way or another, produce a resolution; second, that parties may perhaps try harder to be reasonable and to resolve the matter during the mediation phase; and third, that if an adjudication is required, there will be no loss of time or cost in having to re-acquaint a new neutral with the facts of the case and the issues between the parties. It may have two negative consequences in comparison with mediation. Firstly, if the parties in med-arb feel that a settlement has been imposed upon them – rather than voluntarily agreed to – they may be less willing to comply with it. Secondly, if the parties focus primarily on persuading the mediator that they are right, rather than on seeking an accommodation with the other party, they will not improve their ability to resolve disputes without resort to an outside decision maker. (See Ury, Brett and Goldberg, *Getting Disputes Resolved Designing System to Cut the Costs of Conflict* (1988) Jossey-Bass, San Francisco.)

[7] In a letter dated 8 January 1938 written by Mr. Quentin Hogg to the Lord Chancellor, Viscount Hailsham, Mr. Hogg best expressed the difference between:

> ... the foreign system of 'conciliation' as distinct from the English system of 'arbitration' in commercial contracts. As you are aware, the vital distinction between these two systems is as follows. An English arbitrator, although chosen by the parties, is still a judge in the sense that he must administer the law: in disputes arising out of a contract ... his function is to give effect to the rights of the parties under the contract. He has no right to carve out a new contract or to suggest reasonable or equitable courses ... The Latin system of conciliation is based on a totally different conception. The referee undertakes the good offices of a friend, but his decision, being under the reference, has the binding force of law. He is not limited to decide the dispute according to the rights of the parties, or even to decide who is in the right at all. His object may be equally to effect a compulsory compromise and he may therefore by his award direct the parties to do that to which they have never agreed, and which, apart from the award, they would never have been bound to do...

commercial arbitration of jurists with such different origins has, in practice, caused such inflexible positions to be questioned.[8] In fact, even in continental Europe, procedural laws in countries of Germanic origin included an obligation for the judge to facilitate conciliation between the parties throughout the proceedings. Likewise, in countries of the Far East, conciliation is something natural and closer to the mentality of its jurists than litigation or arbitration. The excessive 'judicialisation' of international commercial arbitration (especially in those proceedings in which jurists from the United States participate) has in fact led to the search for alternative techniques distinct from both litigation and arbitration.

The first question which arises is knowing whether a person who has acted as mediator or conciliator may later intervene as arbitrator in the same conflict and among the same parties. The general rejection which this proposition enjoyed some years ago is today questioned even by the most reticent. It primarily depends on the will of the parties in conflict and the ethcial beliefs of the person whose services are solicited. The parties may even prefer someone who has known a conflict in conciliation to be the person in charge of deciding as arbitrator after the conciliation or mediation attempt has failed.[9] The limits of his performance as

[8] There seems to be a definite diversity in the opinions and the approaches as to how active an arbitral tribunal should be in promoting a settlement and the manner in which exploration of settlement possibilities should be handled. One school of thought sees no difficulty in the transformation of an arbitrator into a mediator and, if necessary, reincarnating him as an arbitrator in the same dispute. Another school of thought has difficulty with this role-changing and feels that settlement negotiations in the nature of a mediation ought to be facilitated by a person different from the arbitrator, so that the arbitrator retains complete independence from the private considerations of each party as to settlement possibilities. Still another school sees no difficulty in the arbitrator becoming a mediator, but feels that, once the mediator role has been assumed, it is not possible for the same person to be born again as an arbitrator required to make an adjudication dispute.

[9] As a matter of fact, companies which actually enter into transnational merger transactions show an increasingly inherent desire to avoid both the escalation of antagonism that the adversarial system has come to represent and the severe financial consequences of corporate litigation. Thus, in contrast to the former long-standing attitude of seeking justice through judicial channels, many of these companies nowadays seek, where practicable, to settle their conflicts through consensus. Hence, alternative dispute resolution (ADR) in merger transactions is needed. The spectrum of available mechanisms briefly falls into two broad categories: binding and non-binding procedures. These devices are not always mutually exclusive, but rather complementary, especially

arbitrator will be established by himself in accordance with his own conscience: in his decision, it seems quite impossible that he may mentally disregard everything which he may have discovered during the conciliation or mediation phase; however, the influence and use during his arbitral

cont.

when applied in merger transactions. Arbitration, combined with other ADR methods, versus litigation: that is the idea. Arbitration and ADR are more economic, more flexible and quicker than litigation. They also meet needs of the business community which judicial litigation cannot: such as confidentiality of the disputes and the expertise in their settlement. Whereas the expertise regarding the analysis of the merits of the case is a clear and settled advantage of ADR methods (notably since it is undeniable that there has been a litigation explosion worldwide which overloads both courts and judges and impedes the specialisation required) confidentiality – especially in arbitration – has become a crucial and disputed factor which the parties to arbitration expect to be really effective. It contrasts sharply with the public nature of litigation. Consequently, it is perceived to be particularly advantageous where a dispute occurs between sophisticated parties in cross-border merger transactions where both parties are anxious to protect and control their priceless confidential material. However, the tailoring of these methods to such intricate transactions demands a great deal of negotiation between contract drafters in order to avoid those problems which are most likely to arise. Draftsmen in merger transactions frequently include mixed or multi-step dispute resolution clauses by means of which any disputes relating to, for example, post-closing balance sheet adjustments shall be resolved by a neutral expert and all others shall be resolved under a more general arbitration provision: in short, an attractive combination of binding and non-binding ADR mechanisms. Among these non-binding alternatives, the retention of a neutral expert (from an established 'big six' accounting firm) is widely used in cross-border merger transactions. The parties may provide that the expert not be of the same nationality as either of the disputants and that he or she possess certain credentials or conform to some set of contractually stipulated criteria. One risk arises, however, when the appointed expert delivers an evaluation in a private session, as the parties may think he is a two-timer who gives both sides the same line about their case being weak. Therefore, the expert has an obligation to present a consistent evaluation on both sides. Usually, the task of these neutral experts is to analyse and settle disputes relating to post-closing balance sheet adjustments, the most common in these type of transactions. Provisions of this nature should specify the appropriateness of the mechanism; tailor the process to the particular problem; be simple and easily accessible and resolve disputes at an early stage and at the lowest organisational level, thus avoiding bureaucracy. Parties who decide to refer disputed issues to an expert should also consider in advance the extent to which the expert's determination will be binding, not only upon them, but also upon an arbitration tribunal.

decision-making process of all that he has discovered is something which only he can determine within the limits of the parties' desires and the applicable rules and legislation.

Another question, similar to the above, rests in knowing whether, in the middle of an arbitration proceeding, the parties may consent to the arbitral tribunal undertaking the functions of a conciliator or mediator.[10] Until very recently, the rejection of this arbitration doctrine was generalised. Today, the answer to this question depends on the will of the parties.[11] It is with them that the arbitral tribunal must establish the terms of the conciliation or mediation period and suspend arbitral activity

[10] In fact, the admissibility and appropriateness for an arbitrator to act as conciliator is among the most controversial issues in arbitration. The differences in the views on this issue clearly have their origin in different legal cultures. Traditionally, a judge in the common law countries is not permitted to be actively involved in settlement facilitation. However, this traditionally hostile attitude to conciliating efforts by the judge and arbitrator is changing (see, for example, Canada, where the new favourable approach finds a clear expression in the 1991 Alberta Arbitration Act, Australia, in the 1990 New South Wales Commercial Arbitration Act, the 1990 Hong Kong Ordinance, the 1994 Singapore International Arbitration Act, the 1993 Bermuda International and Conciliation Act or the 1996 English Arbitration Act). In civil law countries, the position varies. In France (although it is expressly mentioned as one of the functions of the judge or the arbitrator), French arbitration practitioners are reserved to a combination. In Germany, the judge is at any stage of the proceedings bound to see to an amicable settlement of the dispute or any of the contentious issues. A similar provision applies in Austria. In Turkey the combination is allowed for neither the judge nor the arbitrator. Art. 1043 of the 1986 Netherlands Arbitration Act expressly allows settlement efforts by the arbitrators.

[11] What seems important in this area is, once again, respect for party autonomy. Having chosen arbitration, the parties' expectations of an adjudication are basically assured. This does not preclude a tribunal from actively suggesting exploration of settlement, but any such exploration must be voluntarily accepted by, rather than imposed on, the parties, who must also have the power to choose how any settlement explorations are to be conducted. If the arbitrator is to be invested with a mediative function – *amiable compositeur* – and if it is envisaged that the same person may return to the arbitral function, this should be voluntarily and explicitly agreed. Provided that such transparency is respected, party expectations will not be disappointed and arbitration as an institution will be broad enough to accommodate the diversity of psychology that prevails throughout the world in respect to dispute resolution.

during this phase. In the event that the mediation or conciliation is successful, then the parties, by mutual agreement, must decide how this positive result should be formalised: either separately from the arbitration proceedings or as an agreed award by the tribunal.[12] Likewise, they must set the terms under which the arbitration proceedings shall continue if the conciliation or mediation between the parties does not prove possible, establishing these conditions in the clearest possible fashion to prevent challenge of the arbitrator or an eventual appeal of the arbitration award. In any event, it shall likewise be the arbitral tribunal which will decide the ethical limits within which it may use, during the arbitration phase, the information which has been obtained during the conciliation or mediation attempt. The important question may arise as to whether the arbitrator becomes bound in his arbitration decision to the proposal which he may have made during the mediation phase, in the sense that, if under mediation terms he proposes the payment of a specific compensation to one of the parties, may he disregard his mediation proposal or even modify it later on when he makes his arbitration decision after his mediation formula has been rejected.

The arbitrators' interactive approach as a formula to overcome the possible clash of legal cultures shows that the initial dogmatic position of rejecting a combination of arbitration with an eventual mediation or conciliation is not correct, especially when this is what the parties clearly wanted by mutual agreement.

[12] Settlement does not always surprise an arbitrator. Often, the nature of the dispute or certain elements of it, immediately suggest settlement possibilities. The arbitrator may then recommend the parties to attempt to conciliate, a practice which is common in the courts of a number of countries. Thus, in France, courts practice the so-called judicial mediation by means of which the court itself appoints a mediator who discusses the case with the parties outside the court. The mediator later reports on the result without revealing information concerning the content of the mediation or the parties' position. This practice can be applied in arbitration. Clause 10 of the AAA Commercial Arbitration Rules provides for the possibility of mediation during an arbitration procedure, 'mediation window' or *intermezzos* which, although favoured by some, seems to be rarely used in international arbitration. This may be due to the fact that arbitration practitioners are reluctant to make such a suggestion when they are sitting as arbitrators as the parties might not appreciate this from them. The parties engaged in an arbitration logically expect the arbitral tribunal to settle their dispute.

II. COMMUNICATION BETWEEN THE ARBITRAL TRIBUNAL AND THE PARTIES ON MATTERS OF EVIDENCE

An essential point to the smooth development of the arbitration proceedings is the effective communication between the arbitrators and the parties on matters of evidence. It is here that the cultural differences between jurist from different backgrounds truly appear.[13]

Discovery constitutes the true cornerstone in the Anglo-Saxon legal process where even clear differences exist between jurisdictions.[14] This

[13] Evidence refers to proof, testimonies and documents which may legally be presented to prove or disprove a fact under inquiry. In an adversarial procedure such as arbitration, however, evidence is an inquiry in which the parties themselves are responsible for the adduction of evidence. There are four possible types of evidence: (i) direct, where evidence of facts is communicated directly to the court by someone who himself has perceived the fact to be proved; (ii) circumstantial, where the evidence does not directly prove the desired facts, but the existence of proof of those facts can be inferred from it; (iii) real, consisting of material objects other than documents, which are produced for inspection by the arbitral tribunal and which can be either immediate (directly available for perception by the tribunal) or reported (existence is reported by a witness); and (iv) documentary, which could be primary or secondary. In order to avoid the inefficiency of the adversarial procedure, the arbitrator should determine which issues and evidence are important and which are not. Of course, the arbitrator has the duty to exclude offered evidence where it is not relevant, in order to save time and thus guarantee one of the most relevant advantages of arbitration, namely rapidity. There is also an opportunity to rebut adverse evidence. This is an extremely important principle because if people do not know in detail what is alleged against them, a proper defence cannot be prepared. Considering this factor, if a person does not have the opportunity to rebut adverse evidence, the evidence on which a decision is based is significantly incomplete. Even if a decision is correct, without having had an opportunity to rebut all adverse evidence, an adversely affected party might not be convinced that justice has been done and thus the award might be set aside.

[14] In common law countries, an automatic discovery procedure is practised in court actions, under which the parties are obliged to disclose the existence of all relevant documents, whether or not they are favourable to that party's contentions. Discovery is an essential feature of the English adversarial system as it compensates for the tribunal's lack of inquisitorial powers. Properly used, it is a powerful instrument of justice. In cases where all the information relative to a particular event or fact lies in the hands of one party, discovery may provide the only means of ascertaining the truth. On the other hand, if it is employed without discrimination, the procedure can have serious

is one of the most difficult matters to handle when one has to chair an arbitral tribunal between a North American party and another from a

cont.

practical disadvantages. In complex cases, a full order for discovery may require the parties to list and produce large quantities of documents, all but a small fraction of which are of no interest or value to either party. Moreover, an order for discovery takes for granted that both sides will thoroughly comply with the order. If this assumption is falsified and one party gives full discovery while the other does not, the former may be placed at a serious disadvantage. If injustice is to be avoided, the arbitrator must ensure that the process is carried out fairly, if it is to be carried out at all. Mustill and Boyd have described discovery as 'an essential feature of the English adversary system' (Mustill and Boyd *Commercial Arbitration* (2nd edn., 1989) at 324). Under the law as it stood until 1990, if a foreign party was involved in arbitration in England, the arbitrator was required to consider that they may not be familiar with this process, as civil law jurisdictions have very limited exceptions to the general rule that does not provide for any discovery at all. Tribunals in civil law countries have the inquisitorial powers which the English courts lack. This discovery procedure, however, did not apply to arbitration. An arbitral tribunal sitting in England had power to order the parties to produce relevant documents by virtue of the Arbitration Act 1950, s. 12(4). A common misconception is that arbitration in England involves the same degree of discovery as does litigation, the reality being that the extent of discovery is left to the parties to agree. If they choose to have no discovery, then that is binding on the arbitral tribunal (see Croal 'Misconceptions about Discovery in English Arbitration' in (1985) 51 *Arbitration* 539; Hunter 'Arbitration Procedure in England: Past, Present and Future' in (1985) 1 *Arbitration International* 82). In England, it was formerly possible to apply to the court for an order for discovery of documents, but this was abolished in 1990, repealed by the Courts and Legal Services Act 1990, s. 103. Since then, the question of which documents should be produced in an arbitration is entirely a matter for the arbitral tribunal to decide (assuming that the parties have not agreed a procedure for discovery). In fact, nowadays, discovery in arbitration is changing somewhat due to the civil law influence. Hence, under s. 34(d) of the Arbitration Act 1996, it will be for the tribunal to decide whether any, and, if so, which, documents should be produced by the parties. This reflects the actual state of affairs in English arbitration practice because, under the new Arbitration Act, the Tribunal may decide not to order discovery at all, or if so, only in a very limited manner. The practice adopted by arbitral tribunals in common law countries is, therefore, likely to be close to that which is employed in the civil law countries. In the latter, the position is broadly that the arbitral tribunal has discretion to conduct the proceedings in such a manner as it considers fit and to make such procedural rulings as it considers necessary. This type of discretion can be seen as an interaction of civil law with common law arbitration practice and can be found, for example,

Latin American country.[15] While to the North American jurist it seems quite obvious that the other party must reproduce as many documents as may be related to the case under question,[16] the Latin American jurist reacts by presenting exclusively those which may benefit him, feeling legitimately proud of retaining those which in one way or another, may harm him. The arbitral tribunal will be prudent at determining what it will demand from the parties in conflict, supported by the potential sanction that a refusal to present certain adverse presumptions being made against the party reluctant to present relevant evidence.[17]

cont.

under art. 184 of the PILA, which provides that documents on which a party relies are to be filed, together with the pleadings, with the court as an exhibit or attachment. On the other hand, the ICC Rules do not include any specific reference to discovery. In ICC arbitrations, arbitrators do not generally issue orders for the production of documents, usually because they have been produced already in the form of exhibits to the parties' pleadings.

15 See Reymond, 'Common Law and Civil Law Procedure: Which is the More Inquisitorial? A Civil Lawyer's Response' in (1989) 5 *Arbitration International* 357; Staughton, 'Common Law and Civil Law Procedure: Which is the More Inquisitorial? A Common Lawyer Response' in (1989) 5 *Arbitration International* 357.

16 The US discovery system is one of the principal reasons why some potential litigants prefer to agree to arbitration rather than face US Courts. The Federal Arbitration Act and a number of state statutes grant broad discretionary powers to arbitral tribunals to require the production of documents. The general practice in North American litigation is to permit very broad discovery which encompasses not only documents but also the evidence of potential witnesses. There is, however, a similar misconception that arbitrations taking place in the United States are subject to the broad, sweeping discovery procedures available in litigation. The reality is that in the United States there is generally no right to any discovery in arbitrations and the extent to which discovery is permitted is entirely in the hands of the arbitral tribunal if the parties do not agree. As exemplified by *Hunt* v. *Mobil Oil* (1984) 583 F. Supp. 1092 (S.D.N.Y.), the courts will not interfere to extend any right of discovery ordered by the arbitral tribunal. A third party may be subpoenaed to attend the arbitral hearings to give evidence only by a court of competent jurisdiction. Thus, under s. 7 of the Federal Arbitration Act, US Courts will assist the arbitral tribunal in enforcing the attendance of witnesses and hold that third party in contempt if it does not comply.

17 An arbitral tribunal composed of lawyers from civil law countries will rarely make a direct order against a party for the production of documents. However, if one party has made a request to the other for the production of documents, specified with reasonable particularity, and that party has refused to

The preparation of witnesses and experts with a view to their participation in hearings before the arbitral tribunal may equally reflect profound cultural and ethical differences between the parties in conflict. The normal practice – and one which some jurists consider desirable – is to prepare them for this process (including trial performances recorded on video) which may be shocking and even reproachable from the ethical and professional perspective of jurists from a different cultural background.[18] The tribunal must thus know how to distinguish different cultural origins in the evaluation of their respective testimonies.[19]

The practice of cross-examination is the balance established procedurally in some countries and may form the subject of legitimate preparation of witnesses and experts.[20] In other legal systems, however, there is an undeniable allergy towards the aggressive nature of cross-examinations. Even on this point there may be a mixture of different attitudes among

cont.

produce them, the arbitral tribunal will make it clear that it is likely to draw an adverse inference from the refusal to disclose the documents – unless a reasonable excuse is given. In any case, whether discovery is available or not in the legal system in question, an arbitral tribunal lacks the coercive power to order production of documents in the possession of a third party even if such documents may be very relevant to the matters in issue. Any powers that an arbitral tribunal may have to order discovery of documents apply only to the parties to the arbitration.

18 See Hill-Sinicropi, *Evidence in Arbitration* (2nd edn., 1985) BNA Books at 72–75.

19 In international arbitration, the way in which witnesses are examined tends to borrow elements both from the civil law and the common law tradition. Nowadays, because procedure in international arbitration may be governed by foreign practice, witnesses may be examined, cross-examined and re-examined in accordance with common law practice in most European jurisdictions (eg. Switzerland, France and the Netherlands) provided that the parties, the arbitral tribunal or both have jointly included a provision in the arbitration agreement, the terms of reference or a procedural order.

20 Professor Irving Younger put it best when he pointed out that cross-examination 'is the greatest engine ever invented for the discovery of truth' (Younger 'An Irreverent Introduction to Hearsay' in (1977) *ABA* 2) and that it distinguishes a common law trial from a trial under any other legal system. It is simply the examination of a witness by a party that did not call him. The purposes of cross-examination are as follows: (i) to disclose known facts or admissions not related in direct testimony that may contribute independently to the favourable development of your case, (ii) to correct misstatements of facts, (iii) to place facts in true perspective, (iv) to reconcile apparent contradictions and (v) to impeach the reliability and credibility of a witness. Most cross-examinations are directed to this last purpose.

the arbitrators composing the arbitral tribunal as the neutrality and independence of many of them contrast, in some cases, with the partiality and true 'watchdog' function performed by others.[21] One attitude or another shall condition the participation of arbitrators in the cross-examination of witnesses or experts.[22]

[21] The harshest forms of cross-examination would probably not be encouraged by the chairman unless all counsel are from a common law country, simply in order to make sure that the other party is not prejudiced by the resort to a system with which they are unfamiliar.

[22] It is usual for an arbitral tribunal to be given express power to appoint experts if it considers this to be necessary or desirable. Such a power to appoint experts is generally found in the arbitration agreement, either as an expressed term (as in a submission agreement), or through the incorporation of international or institutional rules of arbitration (as in UNCITRAL 1976 Arbitration Rules, art. 27; ICC Rules, art. 14.2; and LCIA Rules, art. 12). In the absence of any express power, the question may arise as to whether or not an arbitral tribunal has an implied power to appoint an expert under the law governing the arbitration. Nevertheless, it is unusual for the applicable law to contain such a power. It is a well-established principle in most systems of national law that, unless expressly authorised to do so by the terms of his appointment, someone to whom a duty has been delegated must not sub-delegate that duty to someone else: *delegatus non potest delegare*. So long as it is plain, however, that the arbitral tribunal is merely taking advice from an expert (rather than attempting to delegate its task to him) it is difficult to find objections to the appointment of an expert by an arbitral tribunal. This principle was cited by the Iran–United States Claims Tribunal, as exemplified in *Starret Housing Corp. et al.* v. *The Government of the Islamic Republic of Iran et al.* (Award number 32-4-1 (19 December 1983), 4 *Iran–US CTR* 122). If an arbitral tribunal needs expert technical assistance in order to understand complex technical matters and needs to understand these matters in order to arrive at a proper conclusion, there is no good reason to prevent it from obtaining such assistance. For example, it has been accepted by the English courts that arbitrators have the right to refer to experts for assistance (*W. Naumann* v. *E. Nathan & Co. Ltd.* (1930) 36 Lloyd's Rep. 268 and 37 Lloyd's Rep. 249) and, in the absence of an express provision, an international arbitral tribunal may generally assume that, provided the law governing the arbitration so permits, it has an implied power to call upon expert assistance when needed. As a corollary to this power, the arbitral tribunal should give the parties an opportunity to comment on any expertise upon which the arbitrators have relied, including their own, if any. This has been clearly established in English law in cases like *Louis Dreyfus & Co* v. *Arunachala Ayya* (1924) 54 Lloyd's Rep. 60; *Threlfall* v. *Fanshawe* (1850) 1 LM&P 340; 19 LJQB 334; 15 LTOS 210; and *Giacomo Costa Fu Andrea* v. *British-Italian Trading Company* (1961) 105 Sol Jo 1068, [1961] 2 Lloyd's Rep.

Fluent communication between the arbitral tribunal, and in particular its chairman, and the parties will assist the arbitrators in ascertaining the facts underlying the dispute which they must arbitrate. An interactive approach in arbitration proceedings can only motivate communication between the arbitrators and the parties to guarantee the general undisputed principles of international due process[23] in the sphere of international arbitration – that is to say, always applying equal treatment to the parties,[24] granting a fair opportunity to present a

cont.

392; on appeal [1963] 1 QB 201; [1962] 2 All ER 53; [1962] 3 WLR 512, 106 Sol Jo 219, [1962] 1 Lloyd's Rep. 151 CA). The selection of an expert or experts and the formulation of his assigned tasks are matters in which the arbitral tribunal may or may not wish to consult the parties as involving the parties may lengthen the process. However, their involvement may have a positive effect by reducing later objections to the expert's report. The measures adopted by the Iran–United States Claims Tribunal in several of its cases are instructive. In naming an expert, the Tribunal first granted the parties the opportunity to agree on an expert and then presented them a list of individuals and institutions from which to choose, stating that if the parties were still unable to agree on a particular expert, the Tribunal would choose the expert itself. Similarly, the Tribunal also sought input from the parties concerning the expert's terms of reference and instructed the expert to submit a preliminary report upon which the parties could then comment. The expert was expected to take these comments into account when preparing his final report. In this way the parties were able to assist the expert in making the report complete, while being reassured that important aspects of the case were not being decided without their involvement.

23 In common law they are known as principles of natural justice: impartiality, opportunity to be heard and grounds for decisions. As Professor David states (David, *Arbitration in International Trade* (1985) Kluwer at 291), in arbitration

> ... the principles in question may be reduced to three. A first principle is *audi alteram partem*: each party must be given the opportunity to be heard. A second one is the principle of contradiction: all elements of proof invoked by a party, and on which the arbitrator is likely to found his decision, must be communicated to the other party, who must be given the opportunity to contradict them. A third principle is that the arbitrator must decide the case on the basis of his own opinion, and not on that of another person ...

24 As to the first two principles – equal treatment of the parties and a fair opportunity to present a case – both international and national legislations world-wide usually link them together (see art. V of the 1958 New York Convention on the Enforcement of Foreign Arbitral Awards; art. 15 of the UNCITRAL 1976 Arbitration Rules; art. 18 of the UNCITRAL 1985 Model Law on International Commercial Arbitration; the ninth headline (para. 2)

case,[25] and fair notice of both the appointment of the arbitrators and the conduct of the proceedings[26] – indispensable elements in the administration of arbitration justice.

III. THE ARBITRATOR'S CULTURAL ORIGIN SHOULD BE IRRELEVANT IN HIS DECISION-MAKING PROCESS

At the beginning of the arbitration proceedings and even before formulating the corresponding claim, the parties in conflict are naturally

cont.
of the Introduction to the Netherlands Arbitration Institute Arbitration Rules in conjunction with its art. 23; art. 15.1 of the Inter-American Commercial Arbitration Commission (Institutional Arbitration Rules); art. 1.694 of the Belgian Judicial Code; art. 1.039 of the Netherlands Code of Civil Procedure; art. 16 of the American Association Rules; art. 14 of the 1988 Nigerian Arbitration and Conciliation Decree; art. 21.1 of 1988 Spanish Arbitration Act; and art. 182.3 of the PILA).

25 In common law, besides an impartial tribunal, the right to a hearing, with special emphasis on notice and opportunity to be heard, is the second requirement of natural justice. This principle includes the right to have adequate notice, to have pre-hearing discovery, to have an adjournment, to present and rebut evidence and to cross-examination of the witnesses and finally, the right to obtain a copy of the corresponding transcript.

26 This principle is extensively regulated in international as well as national arbitration rules world-wide. It is mainly contained in, for example, the American Arbitration Association Rules (arts. 2; 16.2; 19; 21.1; 28.6 and 31.1.); the Euro-Arab Chambers of Commerce Rules of Conciliation, Arbitration and Expertise (arts. 20; 25 and 27.); the ICC Rules of Conciliation and Arbitration (arts. 2.3; 3.3; 4; 6 and 23); the ICSID Rules of Procedure for Conciliation and Arbitration Proceedings (rules 1; 2; 3; 4.5; 5.3; 9.2.b; 30; 31; 42.2; 48; 54 and 55); the LCIA Rules (arts. 1; 2; 4; 10; 16.4 and 17.3.); the Netherlands Arbitration Institute Arbitration Rules (arts. 4; 6.6; 7.1; 7.5; 11.2; 14.1; 15.3; 19.3; 19.7; 20; 22.1; 26.2; 31; 32; 35.3; 41; 50.1.a and 52); the Stockholm Chamber of Commerce Arbitration Rules (arts. 5; 6; 7; 8; 11; 21 and 28); the UNCITRAL 1976 Arbitration Rules (arts. 2; 3; 4; 11; 15; 16.3; 19.1; 24; 25; 27; 28; 29; 30 and 32.6.); the UNCITRAL 1985 Model Law on International Commercial Arbitration (arts. 1; 3 and 24.2.); the Austrian Code of Civil Procedure (art. 592); the Belgian Judicial Code (arts. 1.683; 1.684; 1.702; 1.710; 1.712.2 and 1.716); the 1950 English Arbitration Act (s. 29.2); the Indian Arbitration Act (arts. 14 and 20); the Italian Code of Civil Procedure (arts. 810 and 825); the Netherlands Arbitration Act (arts. 1.058; 1.061; 1.066 and 1.068); the Nigerian Arbitration and Conciliation Decree (arts. 20; 28; 44.3; 44.8; 45 and also arts. 3; 4; 7.2; 15.3; 24; 25 and 27.1 of Schedule I of same); and the 1.988 Spanish Arbitration Act (arts. 22.1; 24; 29 and 33.2).

concerned as to the selection of the arbitrators. This step constitutes a fundamental factor, as the proceeding will be determined by the arbitrator or arbitral tribunal: it is not the same to have an arbitral tribunal chairman or member who is an engineer or a jurist; or who comes from the common law or from the Continent; or who speaks well or passably well the language in which the arbitration proceeding is going to be conducted; or who is familiar or not with the normal practices of the professional sector in which the parties carry out their activities.

However, experience tells us that once the selection is made, arbitrators display their real expertise, and particularly their professionalism, at the time of making their decision, placing aside their individual cultural background. Thus, the truly international arbitrator is one who is immediately able to distinguish what is purely local from that which is outside his own national frontiers and within a globalised economy. His professionalism leads his decision to be independent from the 'bag and baggage' of the system or national systems from which he originates:[27] *da mihi factum et tibi dabo ius*. In his final decision, he is not conditioned by either his geographical origin or his education, his race, his religion or even personal sympathies. Here lies the true professionalism of the international arbitrator who knows how to face the expectations of the parties, who have chosen him for his impartiality and neutrality.

IV. THE POSSIBLE CULTURAL IMPLICATIONS OF THE LOCATION SELECTED FOR THE ARBITRATION PROCEDURE

In many countries, the success of arbitration was delayed until the time when local judges overcame a certain resistance to the competition posed by the arbitrator's activity. Time has made them perceive that arbitrators and judges are in reality partners in the effective administration of justice as desired by the parties in their legitimate use of contractual autonomy.

The fact that the 1958 New York Convention has been ratified by so

[27] In his report for the 1996 ICCA Conference, Guillermo Aguilar Alvarez explained the meaning of the term 'bag and baggage', which includes

... such substantive and procedural rules as a national judge would apply if the dispute had been submitted to the domestic court of one of the parties. In so doing, we recognise that, from a sociological standpoint, bag and baggage probably captures more than just rules of a strict legal nature ...

many countries has been a decisive contribution to the transformation of the judges' initial attitude towards arbitrators from one of confrontation to one of true co-operation. Local judges have applied its rules with the same diligence as they apply ordinary procedural legislation.[28] The fruitful tasks accomplished by the International Council for Commercial Arbitration through its numerous conferences and, more particularly, through the publication of its *Yearbook on Arbitration (*where any national judge can consult on how his colleagues apply the same treaty in other countries) has been an efficient catalyst to the transportation of arbitration's international culture to different and independent national legal cultures. The jurisprudence arising from the application of the New York Convention in local tribunals has unified the interpretation of its different criteria.

We cannot forget the work which numerous institutions in particular UNCITRAL have also accomplished to help bring to different nations the benefit of arbitration.[29] In some cases, it can be described as a

[28] The 1958 New York Convention has been extremely useful in bringing about a uniform standard for the practice of international arbitration. As Mr. Wetter stated, it is 'the single most important pillar on which the premise of international rests' (Wetter 'The Present Status of the International Court of Arbitration of the ICC: An Appraisal' in 1 *American Review of International Arbitration* 91). Further, Lord Mustill said that 'the Convention perhaps could lay claim to be the most effective instance of international legislation in the entire history of commercial law' (Mustill 'Arbitration: History and Background' in 6 *Journal of International Arbitration* 49). According to Redfern and Hunter's opinion (Redfern and Hunter, *International Commercial Arbitration* (2nd edn., 1992) Sweet and Maxwell at 479 *et seq.*)

... at the same time, whilst promoting the 1958 New York Convention as a way of enhancing the effectiveness of arbitration in international trade, it was realised within the UNCITRAL that there was a need for a more unified approach to the basic steps taken in an arbitration ... The aim was to establish a procedural framework which would ensure general international acceptance of the result of the arbitration . . . it was important that the procedure should be suitable for use in both common law and civil law countries, and in the developed and less-developed nations...

[29] The adoption of the 1985 Model Law by States from different parts of the world seems to justify the conclusion that UNCITRAL's initiative in the arbitration field has been favourably received, common law countries being the first to adopt it. As of now, common law and civil law countries have adopted the Model Law in more or less equal numbers. This general acceptance is rather remarkable as the Model Law contains several principles which correspond more with the civil law concept of arbitration than with the common law concept. The Model Law thus may have a harmonising effect.

revolutionary evolution, as in the Hispanic world where arbitration was initially perceived with a certain scepticism due primarily to ideological reasons. Voices had been raised against international commercial arbitration as a threat to the state's sovereignty. Today, however, the acceptance of arbitration in Latin American countries is evidenced by a general ratification of international conventions and a modernisation of the existing arbitration laws.

Collaboration between judges and arbitrators in fact becomes indispensable, in some instances because the drafting of an arbitration clause may be defective or because judicial co-operation may be required to initiate the arbitration procedure. Quite frequently, judges must take provisional measures to guarantee the effectiveness of the arbitration proceeding: either to assist the arbitrator in obtaining material evidence through coercive means or to guarantee effective compliance with the arbitration award at the end of the proceeding. Judges likewise have guardian functions to ensure that the arbitration proceeding is carried out in accordance with the parties' expectations. Similarly, state courts have competence to grant *exequatur* to international arbitration awards or awards rendered in a foreign country. Hence, only state courts may execute by force arbitration awards in the rare case where the parties do not voluntarily execute the award.

Without a doubt, it is in the co-operation between arbitrators and local judges where we are witnessing a greater cultural transformation. International arbitrators have always been closer, and thus more familiar with, the usages and practices of international commercial trade than local judges. However, local judges are co-operating with arbitrators with an ever-increasing international mentality.[30] Their decisions are more frequently being translated and published in foreign countries and this significantly contributes to the internationalisation of their decisions.

[30] The approach followed in the UNCITRAL Model Law and in many countries has been essentially to lay the grounds for the setting aside of an award with those that may justify refusal to enforce it under the 1958 New York Convention. Some countries have gone even further by either excluding any recourse against an international award made there and to be enforced elsewhere or permitting the parties to opt out of such recourse.

V. INTERNATIONAL COMMERCIAL ARBITRATION AS A JUDICAL ANSWER TO THE GLOBALISATION OF THE ECONOMY IN RELATION TO THE RESOLUTION OF INTERNATIONAL COMMERCIAL CONFLICTS

In Toynbee's words we could say that the jurist is permanently receiving challenges from the economy. Today's businessmen are always running ahead of their legal advisers, who are obliged at times to maintain a difficult balance to adopt themselves contractually to their client's requirements.

The most important challenge facing the jurist today is the globalisation of the economy. Educated in a well-known law school of his own geographical corner, he witnesses how economic transactions increasingly surpass his national frontiers, forcing him to adapt archaic and static national criteria to the demands of a growing global economy and its ever more dynamic businessmen.

In a globalised economy, it is thus no longer appropriate to speak of a clash of legal cultures. Arbitrators must transfer the sophisticated *macro* structures to the *micro-economic* relations from which the conflicts being submitted to their decision arise. Today, more than ever, businessmen demand very experienced arbitrators who, through their professionalism, are capable of deciding beyond the cultural barriers of the parties.

Without question, the international private law has substantially changed in content. Few are now interested in the doctrine of the conflicts of law. The jurists have known how to respond effectively to the challenges of the economy's globalisation through the emergence of a true international arbitration culture which demands, in its everyday practice, a more interactive approach to ensure real communication among those who participate in arbitration to meet the expectations of the parties who select this method as the best means to resolve their international commercial conflicts.

Index

STUDIES IN COMPARATIVE CORPORATE AND FINANCIAL LAW

1. Arthur R. Pinto and Gustavo Visentini (eds), *The Legal Basis of Corporate Governance in Publicly Held Corporations: A Comparative Approach* (1998)

2. Betty M. Ho, *Public Companies and their Equity Securities: Principles of Regulation under Hong Kong Law* (1998)

3. Chizu Nakajima, *Conflicts of Interest and Duty: A Comparative Analysis in Anglo-Japanese Law* (1998)
(ISBN 90-411-9698-6)

4. Stefan N. Frommel and Barry A.K. Rider (eds), *Conflicting Legal Cultures in Commercial Arbitration: Old Issues and New Trends* (1999)
(ISBN 90-411-1227-8)

KLUWER LAW INTERNATIONAL – THE HAGUE, LONDON, BOSTON